U.ESS.AY

Politics and Humanity
in American Film

U.ESS.AY

Politics and Humanity
in American Film

Stephen Lee Naish

Winchester, UK
Washington, USA

First published by Zero Books, 2013
Zero Books is an imprint of John Hunt Publishing Ltd., Laurel House, Station Approach,
Alresford, Hants, SO24 9JH, UK
office1@jhpbooks.net
www.johnhuntpublishing.com
www.zero-books.net

For distributor details and how to order please visit the 'Ordering' section on our website.

Text copyright: Stephen Lee Naish 2013

ISBN: 978 1 78279 378 6

Design: Stuart Davies

Printed in the USA by Edwards Brothers Malloy

Mississippi Mills
Public Library

We operate a distinctive and ethical publishing philosophy in all
areas of our business, from our global network of authors to
production and worldwide distribution.

CONTENTS

Acknowledgements

Big thanks to the team at Zero Books. My gratitude to the editors of the journals and magazines in which these essays have appeared: Denise Enck at Empty Mirror Magazine, Alyce Wilson at Wild Violet, Jason Zarri at Scholardarity, Mark Givens at MungBeing Magazine, Jenny & Kate at Versus Literary Magazine, Brentley at Retort Magazine, Monkey Fear at The Fear of Monkeys, and John W. Whitehead and Michael Khavari at Gadfly Online. Friends and former colleagues: Andrew Jury, Dipesh Patel, Mariam Ashraf, Hannah Lenagh-Snow, Neil Anthony Moon, Clare Hardy, Lesley Hammond, Jackie Jarrett. Thank you to Ann-Maureen Owens and Joanne Lalonde for reading over the manuscript and offering helpful guidance. My Family: Mum, Dad, Joanne, Libby and Evie, Gail, Ross and Kara.

This book is dedicated to my wife Jamie, and our son Hayden.

Introduction: Are We Satisfied?

These essays stem from, what I now understand to be, my dissatisfaction with contemporary American cinema. The aesthetics of modern cinema, with its excessive use of computer generated spectacle and lack of substantial narrative has misplaced something valuable and something, perhaps, never to be found again. The sense of realism, excitement and humanity is slowly ebbing away due to the emergence of new technology. When I think back to 2005 and the imminent release of George Lucas's *Star Wars: Revenge of the Sith*, I recall picking over movie magazines and websites that boasted about exclusive on-set photographs, only to be confronted with images of the film's stars Hayden Christensen or Ewan McGregor looking concerned and battle scared in front of vast screens of blue and green. The cinematic still frame, which generated excitement, intrigue and in poster form adorned countless bedroom walls, was lost. My disappointment with the emergence of digital cinema was well entrenched from this point onward. Directors, it appeared, were intentionally dispensing with realism and incorporating unnatural landscapes and non-human elements into the productions. This came to a zenith in 2010 with James Cameron's monolithic and mind-blowing 3D, CGI extravaganza *Avatar*, which operated within the completely computer generated world of Pandora. Coming away from *Avatar* audiences began feeling a tinge of post-Avatar blues, a longing to return to the lush green forests and burning blue skies of Pandora, an impossible dream to realize. This is witness to a new form of dissatisfaction, not just with cinema as such, but with our modern lives. Perhaps this is why contemporary cinema has become so obnoxious and overblown; we want our escapism to be as far apart from the real world as possible, and that entails creating new ones that appear to be unattainable utopias. However far filmmakers like George Lucas and James Cameron go to create such elaborate and believable worlds, we will never be fully satisfied, and neither will they. George Lucas is constantly tinkering with his creations, integrating CGI characters within the conversations of the original live-action and vehicles and space ships into the original stop-motion action; although the sale of his empire to Disney in 2013 might mean he no longer has the right to do this. James Cameron is in preparation for *Avatar 2* and plans an even bigger spectacle of mind blowing/numbing visuals. This isn't to suggest that all digitally produced films are like this. On the flipside of the digital revolution the last decade has seen independent film once again find an outlet, which has been opened up by the accessibility and cheapness of domestic digital film technology. The emergence of the Mumblecore movement as a sub genre within independent American filmmaking is challenging and commenting socially on our modern times and portraying a more realistic and humanistic slice of life, but however satisfying and real these films might be, they are continually drowned out by the noise and bluster of modern blockbusters.

Within all art exists a form of reaction, and the films covered in this book are reactive to the times and culture in which they were produced; although in some cases this may not at all be obvious. Why for example in a book that covers American cinema are there two essays on North Korea? Arguably, North Korea is one of the most reactionary nations in the world. Its entire existence is based upon reaction to, what it perceives as, imperialism and empire, first from Japan, its previous occupier, and now from America, its current antagonist. North Korea's cinematic endeavours are striving to be on par with American film, whilst also peddling the country's socialist propaganda to the masses. North Korea, however, is not alone in doing so. What this collection of articles attempts to elucidate is that American cinema is just as potent with nationalism, manipulation of historical fact, use of distraction and spectacle, and extrapolation of a capitalist ideal as the North Koreans are with their ideal of 'socialism'.

Commando, Arnold Schwarzenegger and US Foreign Policy

During the 1980s American jingoism was at its most potent, due largely to the flexing of political and economic muscles against the Soviet Union during the last decade of the Cold War, when America was fast becoming the unmistakable winner of the long running conflict. After a deep recession in the early eighties, the American economy bounced back with persistent growth throughout the decade, and its dominance of popular culture, film, television, music and produce spread worldwide. America was thought to be the shining beacon and template of democracy and economic stability throughout the world. In Hollywood, producers and studios fell over themselves to provide the clearest and most robust outlook of American power. Action films, the decade's definitive film genre, portrayed American film stars as bulletproof, muscle-enhanced avenging angels. The decade's two main action stars who were most representative of this era were Austrian-born, former Mr. Universe, Arnold Schwarzenegger, and the son of Italian immigrants, Sylvester Stallone. Both were living embodiments of the American Dream, raising themselves from humble beginnings to conquer the entertainment industry and later, in Schwarzenegger's case, the political landscape. America's attitude towards foreign countries and its own foreign policy was echoed in eighties action movies like Stallone's *Rambo* Trilogy (1982, 1985, 1988) and Schwarzenegger's *Commando* (1986) and *Predator* (1987). The suave assertion of these films was that despite various violent interventions against its perceived enemies, America remained irreproachable and its actions legitimate under the circumstance of foreigners gone rogue. In these narratives, America had to be the player to put everyone right.

In the film *Commando,* Arnold Schwarzenegger plays retired

Delta Force operative Colonel John Matrix. Matrix and his teenage daughter Jenny live a secluded, peaceful life in the mountain ranges of California. That peace is shattered when Matrix's former superior General Franklyn Kirby arrives by helicopter and informs him that his old military unit has been killed off one by one. Kirby leaves Matrix with two commandos as protection. As soon as Kirby's helicopter is out of sight Matrix is attacked by hidden mercenaries. Easily dispensing with the two commandos, the group of mercenaries kidnap Jenny. Matrix gives chase, but is overcome and shot with a tranquilizer by one of his former-commando-buddies-turned-traitor, Bennett (Vernon Wells). When he awakes in chains, his captor is revealed to be Arius (Dan Hedaya), the former dictator of fictional South American country Val Verde, who Matrix once helped to overthrow in a coup and in his place installed the country's new leader President Velasco (itself a possible reference to José María Velasco Ibarra, five times president of Ecuador, or Juan Francisco Velasco Alvarado, the left-wing General and President of Peru who lead a bloodless military coup to overthrow Fernando Belaúnde Terry in 1968). With Matrix's daughter in captivity, Arius blackmails him into assassinating President Velasco in order for Arius to return to power in a proposed military coup. Matrix reluctantly agrees to travel to Val Verde and kill the President. Arius deems it a fitting punishment that Matrix should have to destroy the regime he helped to create, and mockingly reminds Matrix of his friendship with Velasco, and the honorific of 'hero of the revolution' bestowed upon Matrix after the coup. However, in true action hero fashion, just as he has boards the plane for Val Verde, Matrix kills his chaperone, and jumps from the plane as it is taking off. With 11 hours before the plane arrives in Val Verde, Matrix sets about trying to find his daughter and kill former-dictator Arius.

There is little need to continue the narrative beyond this point. This being a 1980s American action film it is obvious that Matrix succeeds in his mission to rescue his daughter and dispense with the bad guys in an indiscriminately violent fashion (entire military units of Arius army are dispassionately slaughtered, while Matrix murders Arius henchmen with classic one-liners). This is typical of American action films of the Republican Reagan and Bush administrations. The excessive use of indiscriminate force on screen reflects a broader self-justification for an invasive and domineering Foreign Policy in reality. The Reagan administration's own doctrine orchestrated and supported uprisings against countries that had fallen under the spell of the communist Soviet Union. The Reagan Doctrine was designed to weaken the global influence of the Soviet Union and to heighten the dominance of America during the Cold War. Hollywood action films appear to have become the Republicans' propaganda machine of choice.

Although we know nothing solid of the fictional country of Val Verde, its use as a stereotypical South American template speaks volumes about American ignorance towards its southern neighbors and the desires of its peoples (the short glimpse of Val Verde is that of a typically poor and rundown market district patrolled by armed army officers, in the background we see posters of Arius with red crosses scrawled over his face). Although we assume that the former dictator Arius was not a popular or democratically elected leader (the fact that he wants to take the country back by force and has kidnapped Matrix's daughter to do so would seem to support this), we can safely draw the conclusion that Arius was hugely unpopular with the American government. So unpopular in fact that they authorized a delta force unit to help overthrow Arius and install a puppet leader who was friendly to American interests. This echoes all too much America's history of intrusive Foreign Policy and its attempts to remove from power democratically elected or popular leaders.

The most obvious examples of this from Latin America and

South America are that of Cuba and Chile. Cuba was drawn into revolution from 1953 to 1959. The populist movement was led by the charismatic outspoken lawyer turned revolutionary Fidel Castro, against the tyrannical US-backed Dictator Fulgencio Batista. Castro was hugely popular with the Cuban people who had suffered great hardship and exploitation under Batista's iron rule. Their land had been pillaged by American corporations and capitalist greed, as well by the hedonistic tourists who lapped up the cheap booze and took advantage of the rampant prostitution and gambling. Cuba was seen as a playground for the exploitative elite. All this changed when the revolution was victorious. Castro swept into power with social programmes and land reforms which nationalized all foreign owned property within the first year in power, a move which brought into effect a trade embargo, which remains to this day, put in place by America against Cuba. Since the revolution, the American Central Intelligence Agency (CIA) has attempted, unsuccessfully, over six hundred times to dispense with Castro in the most ingenious ways (exploding cigars) and has trained anti-Castro operatives to engage in acts of dissent and even full scale invasions, most famously the American backed Bay of Pigs invasion of 1961.

In Chile, the democratically elected Marxist leader Salvador Allende shot himself in the head in 1973 as a US backed coup swept through the country, the foundations of which had been laid earlier by the Richard Nixon/ Henry Kissinger administration just prior to Nixon's election victory in 1970. The desire to keep communist influence at bay was of upmost importance during the Cold War. Although a figure such as Fidel Castro never rose to power democratically or through electoral politics as such, his popularity with the majority of Cuban people was enough to give him and his revolution legitimacy in the eyes of Cuba, its neighbors and the world. Salvador Allende was a different case altogether. His democratic election win was seen by the people of Chile as a step towards taking a truly independent path that would allow them to construct their own future. American interference in Chile's political system meant that the military action to overthrow Allende left the country to be ruled by a junta, lead by the fascistic Dictator General Pinochet, who after gaining power banned all left-wing parties and literature, and instigated a regime of terror that led to a total number of torture victims of approximately 40,018, including 3065 killed for political reasons.[1]

Hollywood would like its audience to believe that its depiction of foreign intervention by the US government is righteous. By using tired clichéd caricatures of bogus dictators, Hollywood paints a picture that it is acceptable to remove these supposed despots from power by force, and put a more moderate figurehead in their place. In reality, this is rarely the case. As for Arnold Schwarzenegger, during the more liberal Clinton years, Schwarzenegger's image softened somewhat, allowing or perhaps pushing him into starring in comedies such as *Junior* (1994) and *Jingle all the Way* (1996) as well as action movie parodies like *Last Action Hero* (1993). The return of the Republican Party in 2000 with the narrow election victory of George W Bush saw Schwarzenegger revisit harder game with science fiction/action film *End of Days* (1999) and horror movie *The Sixth Day* (2000), and of course his third outing as the Terminator in *Terminator: Rise of the Machines* (2003). By this point, however, Schwarzenegger's acting days were coming to an end, yet his turn towards politics was perhaps the best performance of his career. Merging his past characters' repertoire of catchy one-liners and his own charming personality, Schwarzenegger was elected to the role/position of the Republican Governor of California on November 17, 2003. In a way the conservative political path Schwarzenegger took was obvious. His films celebrated patriotism and gleefully indulged in violence towards outsiders, even though at some points in conservative American politics his immigrant status would have been one of the targets. In an address to the Republican Convention in 2004 he stated: "To think that a once scrawny boy from Austria could grow up to become Governor of the State of California and then stand here – and stand here in Madison Square Garden and speak on behalf of the President of the United States. That is an immigrant's dream! It's the American dream."[2] Arnold Schwarzenegger has lived, breathed, served and, on film at least, he has fought for America's position in the world.

Published in *The Fear of Monkeys*, April 2013

The Night-time Metropolis on Film

In daylight, the cities we inhabit take on a very different function and feel to that of night-time. At sunrise, the city becomes a place of labour and socialization, of culture and community. The constant movement of raucous transportation and talkative commuters offers a distraction to the surroundings and an immersion into the frantic flow of the city. Our senses become numbed by the intense over-stimulation that the squeal of subway trains, the hum of tall buildings, the exhaust fumes of continuous traffic and the hustle that crowds of people provide. When we return to the relative quiet of our homes, we are left emotionally raw, wired and bruised, yet eager to return and face it again. When the night descends and the workers, students, and commuters leave the city behind, another breed of inhabitants emerge into the darkness. People who were perhaps there all along during the daytime hours, but so blurred into the background noise as to be invisible. The city at night is an altered state where the flashing and changing advertisement displays, which were are only glimpsed in the daylight, now buzz and shine their neon glow menacingly onto the street below. In film, the night-time metropolis is deemed to be malevolent and sinful, a place where nothing good could ever happen. In the films *Collateral* (2004), *Cosmopolis* (2012), and *Drive* (2011) the normal inhabitants of the city disappear and are replaced by sinister misfits and degenerates. The vibrant mood and fast pace of the city by day is traded at night for unhurried and deliberate menace and violence.

The city at night has held great appeal to filmmakers for decades. The use of the city as an ominous character within the film came to fruition in the seventies with films such as *Taxi Driver* (1977) and *The Warriors* (1979). In these two films the metropolis is a neon-lit cesspit where the threat of violence and paranoia lurks around every corner. The darkness reflects the internal struggle and conflicts of the characters, and this internal mood is projected externally to the cityscape. Moreover, capitalism itself has made the city an even more segregated environment. The monolithic glass skyscrapers, plush hotels, bars and restaurants that have risen up at alarming rates throughout the world reflect the glossy, flashing billboards that create an ever-changing and inconsistent landscape below. At night the wealthy and affluent population lock themselves within these ivory towers, behind bulletproof glass and many floors above street level. The young and successful fill the nightclubs and bars that muscular bouncers guard from undesirables. The streets are left to the underclass.

Collateral, directed by Michael Mann, defines the mechanisms of the working city. In the day, the sun shines brightly, a sense of restless energy and positivity is apparent. People are in constant transit. However, when Jamie Foxx's taxi driver, Max, heads towards downtown LA as dusk creeps in, a dark looming cloud hovers over the glimmering city, foretelling impending doom for Max and his passenger, a young female lawyer who gives Max her number as he drops her off downtown. That impending doom arrives in the form of Vincent (a silver haired Tom Cruise), a merciless hit man making five consecutive assassinations over the course of the night. Max is reluctantly dragged into the murder spree when Vincent's first hit does not go according to plan and the body of a lowlife criminal falls two stories from a shabby apartment block onto the top of Max's cab. The next few hours are spent in transit as Max ferries Vincent from hit to hit, until Max loses his cool, tosses Vincent's satchel containing his hit list over a bridge and crashes the cab just before the last hit. When Max discovers the last hit is the young female lawyer he took downtown earlier, he sets out to save her life and repent for facilitating Vincent's gruesome crimes. The Los Angeles that Vincent and Max encounter is a jungle of concrete and glass, a neon-lit hell. The menacing red glow of smog hangs over the inner city casting a deadly light over the inhabitants. From above, the city resembles an open wound, the streetlights and cars create an illusion of blood pumping through the veins of a vicious creature. It's obvious that Vincent would choose to make his hits at night, not only to cover his own crimes, but also because the lowlifes and informers he's contracted to kill only come out at night, along with the other degenerates of the city. As the night progresses Max attempts to disrupt Vincent's work and eventually stands up to Vincent as the daytime arrives. They face-off with Vincent dying from a bullet wound on the Los Angeles subway and he is left to ride the train towards the commuters who will soon be boarding. Max and his companion emerge from the darkness of the subway station into the blistering morning daylight.

Although the character of Driver (Ryan Gosling) in *Drive* is not a criminal as such, his association as a getaway driver for robberies is a night-time endeavour. Here the city is presented as a derelict sprawl; the landscape is expansive, with concrete, windowless warehouses and factories lining up along the dimly lit and deserted streets. Driver is a recluse in the same sense that Travis Bickle from *Taxi Driver* is a recluse. Like Bickle, Driver's interactions with people are awkward and guarded; he lives so much within his own mind that other people do not really register. Perhaps the city he inhabits is a bustling metropolis, but his world is so internal that the commotion of everyday life is not on his radar. When he does drop his guard and begins a friendship with his neighbour Irene (Carey Mulligan) and her young son Benicio, he permits himself a weakness that will be eventually exploited. When Irene's husband returns from prison and is badly beaten by his former associates, Driver agrees to help with a robbery that will seal a debt and keep Irene and Benicio safe from harm. The robbery takes place during the daytime and goes horribly wrong (an example reiterating that criminals should only operate at night). Driver's accomplices get shot, although he makes it away with the bag of cash. Driver gets caught up in a criminal underworld that he doesn't understand and wants no part of. He intends to return the stolen money to the mob bosses, an honest move that the bosses can't comprehend. Unfortunately the only exit from the depths Driver has descended into is death. He is stabbed by the mob boss and takes the last moments of his life to drive the streets of LA whilst bleeding from his wounds.

In David Cronenberg's *Cosmopolis* the city is seen from the moving window of young billionaire Eric Packer's sound-proof stretch limousine as an anti-capitalist protest sweeps over the city. *Cosmopolis* represents the rottenness of capitalism within the city. Packer is a cold and calculating financial speculator travelling across Manhattan to get a haircut from his favourite barber. Although a very real threat has been placed on his life by an apparent anti-capitalist extremist, he seems unconcerned and continues his journey with regular updates on his safety coming from his personal bodyguard. Packer's isolation from the world is so apparent that he takes business meetings in his car along the way. When anti-capitalist protestors spray paint and bombard his limo with dead rats, and at one point a demonstrator sets themselves alight with petrol, Packer and his Chief Advisor (Samantha Morton) do not so much as bat an eyelid at the vandalism and suicide they witness. The city Packer inhabits is soundless and isolated. In the evening when he sits in a upscale restaurant with his new wife, who is as cold and isolated from the rest of the world as he is, he comments that the protestors have vacated the city, an example perhaps that the ordinary people have left, or have been hustled away from the city that is now left to the criminals. He also confesses to his wife that his business deals have turned sour and his company is now haemorrhaging money. Packer himself descends into violence and criminality as his capitalist world collapses around him. He coldly and abruptly kills his bodyguard and confronts Benno Levin, the man who is trying to kill him (Paul Giamatti). Levin, as it turns out is former employee of Packer's company, and places the blame of the world's economic insatiability on Packer's head. Levin stands behind a passive and emotionless Packer with a loaded gun to Packer's head. The film ends, but we assume Levin pulls the trigger.

Although capitalism plays a major part of the narrative in *Cosmopolis*, demonstrating the zenith of wealth and greed gone sour, its effects are also apparent in the films *Collateral* and *Drive*. The Los Angeles that Vincent and Max cruise through is awash with unfettered wealth, and on the flip-side, hardship and crime. The economic divide is exemplified by Vincent and Max's brief relationship. To the sophisticated Vincent, Max is a lowly taxi driver who he can bribe with the promise of a night earning a large amount of money; whilst Max initially views Vincent's charm and sophistication as something to which he aspires. In *Drive*, the city is derelict with abandoned windowless factories and cramped and dingy living quarters. This area of the city reflecting the consequence of factory jobs being shipped to foreign countries, making the streets a lonely and desolate place to be. The city at night is a treacherous place for the three protagonists of *Collateral*, *Cosmopolis* and *Drive*. They mingle or align themselves with the criminal underworld and descend into an even murkier underbelly of violence and murder that eventually leads to their own demise. Much like the mythical vampire, who roams the night in search of blood and vice, but must return to the crypt as daytime arrives, these characters cannot be allowed to survive in the daytime. As time runs out for Vincent, Eric and Driver they face their own mortality. The city is literally the death of them.

Published in *Wild Violet*, June 2013

How Dennis Hopper Conquered the American Century

Dennis Hopper's extensive filmography is filled with an array of painfully bad films. His early career saw him appear in any number of B-Movies and exploitation flicks; his late eighties/early nineties excursion into mainstream blockbusters such as *Super Mario Bros* (1993) and *Waterworld* (1995) were undeniably poor; and from the late nineties and beyond, his backlist of movies throw up an assortment of forgettable direct to video/DVD and television movies. Despite this, Dennis Hopper was a legendary and much respected actor, director and artist; his poor acting decisions did not tarnish his status, and even the films which should, in theory, be banished forever, are worth a screening for the scenes in which Hopper fleetingly appears. His reputation remains intact for a simple reason. He appeared in, or in some cases, even directed five films that defined the decades of the last fifty years of the twentieth century. These five films epitomize the times in which they were made, reflecting both, socially and politically, five distinct eras, and reflecting also, the ever changing circumstances of Dennis Hopper's life.

The Fifties: *Rebel Without a Cause*

In 1955, and still an unknown in Hollywood circles, Hopper was cast as a thuggish gang member in the seminal teenage rebellion film *Rebel Without a Cause*. This was not a Dennis Hopper movie; it was very much a vehicle for the immaculately cool James Dean. Whilst Hopper's young hoodlum Goon may not be important within the context of the film, the influence that James Dean asserted on the young Hopper had an immense impact on the rest of Hopper's film and artistic career. Dean introduced

17

Hopper to Method Acting, a realist form of artistic expression that Hopper devoutly continued to follow for his entire career.

Following James Dean's untimely death, Hopper sought to refine his acting technique and by the late fifties began to study under the renowned acting tutor Lee Strasberg in New York. Hopper, in effect, seized the artistic career of which Dean was robbed, making him stubbornly determined to utilize the Method at every opportunity. Because of this, he became a nightmarish prospect to direct, and accordingly, was ousted from mainstream Hollywood and left to wander the wilderness of B-Movies and biker flicks. That is, until one particular biker film changed cinema.

The Sixties: *Easy Rider*

The sixties seemingly brought to America a never ending summer of good drugs and free love. In reality, the decade was a complex game of war and peace; life and death, hope and hopelessness. The Age of Aquarius was drowned out by the gunshots that killed Rev. Martin Luther King JR, President John F Kennedy and his younger brother Senator Bobby Kennedy. In 1962 the world was almost obliterated by the nuclear posturing of the Soviet Union and America, with the Cuban missile crisis threatening to turn the stalemate of the Cold War into a heated conflict. American involvement in the Vietnam War escalated, but socially the decade made some progress. African-American civil rights movements, gay rights and women's rights began to be seriously addressed. The decade is fondly remembered, but carries with it a great deal of societal baggage.

The movie that perfectly captured this schism was *Easy Rider* (1969). *Easy Rider* stands as a milestone in American New Wave cinema. The film allowed the New Hollywood ethos of auteur movie making to fully mature. The narrative of two hippie drifters chasing and failing to grasp the America Dream spoke volumes about where America was at, and, where it was heading. Despite the quest for freedom, *Easy Rider's* undertone personifies the improbability of living in a truly free society. Against this dour subtext, the film's visual beauty and vibrant color make the heart ache with joy. The soundtrack, which incorporated popular rock and folk songs of the time, works as a cultural commentary to the visuals and mood of the film.

Dennis Hopper instantly knew that the sixties' utopian vision was a lie, and *Easy Rider* reflects this as the character of Wyatt (Peter Fonda) regretfully admits that "we blew it". Within the internal framework of the film, what they really blew was their own ideals and principles, but in a social context Wyatt/Fonda is aiming his words at his own generation who had a shot at creating a new enlightened world but didn't have the courage to see it through. *Easy Rider* told the audiences in no uncertain terms that world had become a nightmare.

The Seventies: *Apocalypse Now*

The Seventies saw *Easy Rider's* cultural predictions come true, and Dennis Hopper's role as the jittery photojournalist in the epic *Apocalypse Now* (1979) was the definition of a sixties' burnout. Loosely based on Joseph Conrad's novel *Heart of Darkness*, director Francis Ford Coppola transferred the setting from the colonial Congo of the late nineteenth century to war ravaged Vietnam in the late sixties. Martin Sheen's protagonist, Captain Benjamin Willard journeys the Nung River in search of Marlon Brando's once distinguished, but now completely insane, Colonel Kurtz. After a few hours of Sheen's philosophical voice over, erratic gunfire and a surreal scene involving Playboy bunnies, the film comes to a standstill outside of Kurtz's imperial compound and Hopper's hyperactive photojournalist makes his grand entrance with the superb line: "I'm an American!"

What Hopper achieves with this minor role is inspired. He

violates the screen with his rapid-fire, thousand-thoughts-a-second ranting and raving, his expressive hand movements forcing the audience to comprehend every last syllable of pseudo philosophical rambling. Hopper adds an injection of lunacy that invigorates the film. The photojournalist distils the utter madness of war, and he is in essence the very definition of post-traumatic stress disorder. Hopper's character is haunted by war and conflict, and his escape from frontline reportage has meant that now the war is internal. This was true of Hopper himself, whose ravaged and glassy-eyed appearance was reflective of an internal conflict with drug and alcohol abuse. There is no distinct line drawn between actor and character. Both are one and the same.

The Eighties: *Blue Velvet*

After a number of years ostracized by Hollywood, a newly clean and sober Dennis Hopper made a triumphant return. Hopper's performance of seething anger and childish brutality in *Blue Velvet* (1986) announced to all and sundry that he was back in rude form. Set in the small leafy American suburb of Lumberton, Frank Booth's chilling appearance reveals a dark and dangerous underbelly of American society that the naïve, voyeuristic teenager Jeffrey Beaumont (Kyle McLachlan) descends into. Films of the eighties often portrayed teenagers as over-privileged rich kids, whose lust for danger never seemingly had lasting consequences. Even the supposed delinquent kids in films such as *The Breakfast Club* (1985) and *Ferris Bueller's Day Off* (1986) came from relatively middle-class happy homes and eventually achieve redemption in the eyes of their peers and elders. Jeffrey Beaumont would ultimately pay the price for all those mischievous adolescents of the eighties era. Jeffrey's coming of age would be a devastating loss of innocence. This loss would be at the hands of Frank Booth's psycho-sexual impulses. *Blue Velvet* allowed a change in perspective for audiences who embraced the avant-garde ideals of David Lynch and those that would follow.

The Nineties: *Speed*

The one negative to *Blue Velvet's* excellence is that from this point onward, Dennis Hopper was stereotyped into roles which required him to menace and yell at high decibels. This pigeon-holing is encapsulated in the nineties action blockbuster *Speed* (1994). *Speed* served to redefine the action film genre. Whilst the eighties action film claimed a fantastical, unreal element, with films such as *Terminator* (1984) and *Predator* (1987) containing otherworldly dangers to be vanquished by seemingly super-human and ultra-fit heroes, the nineties brought in a more realistic, gritty action film, steeped in the everyday mundane and relishing in the pre-millennium anxieties of ordinary people.

Hopper's character as a once-honest-bomb-disposal-expert-turned-terrorist, Howard Payne, is no stretch for Hopper's Method acting skills. However, it threads perfectly with the generic persona of action movie bad guys. The unseemly evil intent of world domination or revenge is neither properly explained nor justified: these guys are just bad, plain and simple, and that means they have to be stopped by the good guys, no matter the cost to the cities they often demolish, and the innocents they indiscriminately kill, in order to snare them. *Speed* works because it is executed right and played for dumb kicks; it is not high art and perhaps not *the* definitive film of the nineties, but it certainly operates within the definitive genre and should be counted as a significant piece of modern cinema.

Dennis Hopper defined the post-war American century by embodying the essence of each decade and weaving a thread throughout his career of the collapsing American dream. The young and impressible fifties teenager turned on by drugs, rock 'n' roll music and sex, leads to the buoyant hippie of the sixties embracing the utopian dream of free love, peace and understanding, but ultimately realizing the ideal is unobtainable. This disillusion leads to the bewildered and damaged relic of the seventies, engaged in useless and unwinnable conflicts. And when it is truly understood that such conflicts are unwinnable, this leads to a self-serving sociopath and an indulgent quest for power over people. Then finally the maniac, hell bent on destruction for what life did not give him.

Published in *Empty Mirror*, December 2012

The *Easy Rider* Paradox

It is almost impossible to write and discuss Dennis Hopper and his movies without exploring the cultural and social significance of *Easy Rider*. The impact this small film had on the subsequent decades of filmmaking is immeasurable. We are still feeling the wave rippling today in independent cinema throughout the world. Although the era that *Easy Rider* explores has now perhaps passed by today's generation, the do-it-yourself aesthetic is still relevant to many filmmakers who wish to distance themselves from the Hollywood system, as well as equivalent studio systems, and maintain their independence and keep their artistic vision intact. *Easy Rider* meant many things to many different people from all kinds of social backgrounds and the film addressed a wide scope of subjects relating to its time and place. But what did *Easy Rider* mean to Dennis Hopper? By all accounts *Easy Rider* meant everything to him. His willingness to discuss and dissect his own movie has meant that there are hours of recorded interviews, documentaries, as well as pages and pages of articles and critiques that explore the phenomenon of *Easy Rider*. One interesting aspect of Hopper's post *Easy Rider* career is his incessant need to reference and refer to *Easy Rider* in other films in which he has appeared. One could point out that this is a strange blip in the filmic universe, a paradox of reality and fiction that is only unique to Dennis Hopper.

This phenomenon first became apparent to me in the 1990 comedy film *Flashback*. In this film Hopper plays the character of Huey Walker, a sixties activist and hippie throwback, who, for the past twenty years, has been on the run from the FBI who want to indict him for a childish prank of social disobedience that embarrassed the then Vice President Spiro Agnew, while he toured the United States in the late sixties. Now in the late eighties, the Feds finally catch up with him and place him in the custody of young and uptight FBI agent John Buckner (Kiefer Sutherland). When we first meet Huey Walker, it is almost as if we are meeting *Easy Rider's* Billy twenty years down the line. The character shares the same tussled long hair, bushy beard and fidgety mannerisms that defined Billy's erratic personality. Of course we as an audience know this can't be Billy, Billy is dead, shot by a redneck from the side of a truck. So who is Huey Walker? A relative of Billy or perhaps a ghost, most certainly he is a caricature of Hopper's own perceived personality from that era. The plot thickens, and the merging of the two films becomes more apparent. The captured Walker and the straight-laced fed Buckner travel cross country by train. Over dinner Huey jokes that he has spiked Buckner's food with a tab of acid. Buckner becomes paranoid and panics, drinking copious amounts of booze from the carriage bar to counter the effects of the acid trip. However, there is no acid; Huey has tricked Buckner into getting wasted and losing his otherwise ice-cold persona, thus giving Huey a chance to escape.

Back in their train compartment, Huey shaves his beard, cuts his hair and steals Buckner's sharp suit and FBI badge. He now looks like a typical FBI agent, slick and sharp suited. Buckner passes out on the floor; Huey dresses him in his own ragged old clothes. They make an overnight stopover in a small town where Huey meets the local sheriff and hands over a passed out Buckner to his officers for a stay in the local jail. Huey walks the town and ends up in a bar where two middle aged, middle-class guys are drinking lots of beer and reminiscing about the good old days of the sixties and the weirdness of the eighties. Huey sparks up a conversation with them about their rebel credentials and asks if they remember the activist Huey Walker. He informs them that Huey Walker has in fact been caught and his rotting in the jail across the street. The two ex-hippies are furious, Walker plays up to his new image of obnoxious FBI agent and ridicules them, delivering the line: "*It takes more than going down to your local video store and renting Easy Rider to be a rebel"*, to which one of them replies *"I happen to own Easy Rider"*. As a viewer, ones does the inevitable double take on what was just said by Hopper's character. What are we seeing here? How could the character of Huey Walker have seen *Easy Rider*, without seeing himself in the role of Billy? It's as if a parallel universe, admittedly a filmic parallel universe, has come into existence, one in which Dennis Hopper, Billy and Huey Walker exist in the same world, but as separate individuals. That the two ex-hippies don't even acknowledge the fact that Huey strikes a remarkable resemblance to one of the main characters of *Easy Rider* defies belief. However shameless it appears, Hopper uses *Easy Rider* as a cultural reference point in order to define the sixties era to the younger audience, after all no piece of cinema illustrates that period quite like *Easy Rider*. As the old saying goes *Flashback* is 'only a movie' and that would be an acceptable argument if it wasn't for the fact that Hopper returns to this paradox again and again.

In the 1977 Wim Wenders directed film, *The American Friend* (Der Amerikanische Freund), Hopper plays Tom Ripley a wealthy American art dealer living in Hamburg, Germany, who befriends a dying local picture framer Jonathan Zimmermann (Bruno Ganz). During the first hour of the movie, while standing on the balcony of his plush rented house Tom Ripley, with wireless radio by his ear begins to bellow out *The Ballad of Easy Rider*, one of *Easy Rider's* signature songs, that was written for the soundtrack by Bob Dylan and performed by The Byrds front man Roger McGuinn. As Ripley sings the lyric "Where ever that river flows that's where I want to be" he opens out his arms and embraces the city below him. It's an odd moment in an otherwise faultless film. Hopper's use of the song in no way fits into the mould of the film. Tom Ripley is a character adapted from the 1974 novel *Ripley's Game* by Patricia Highsmith, and in no way is he any sort of ex hippie or former sixties activist. Hopper plays the character of Tom Ripley very differently from the book versions, making him less emotionally detached and distant and giving Ripley an essence of regret and ethics that the literary character disregards. He also plays Ripley as very much in tune with his Americanism; something the Ripley of the novels abandons in order to embrace European values. The use of *The Ballad of Easy Rider* could be to mirror co-star Bruno Ganz's random humming of old Beatles songs. Much like *Easy Rider,* The Beatles were a defining phenomenon of the sixties music and cultural scene. Dennis Hopper's use *of The Ballad of Easy Rider* does not distract from the narrative as it does in *Flashback.* Hopper's interpretation of Tom Ripley allows the character to have a conscience and a genuine feeling of friendship towards Jonathan. Hopper and Ripley's use of the line could be seen as a longing to be free of the murky underworld and that Ripley inhabits.

A very brief example of Hopper's referencing of *Easy Rider* is in the eighties teen flick *My Science Project* (1985), a bizarre little sci-fi oddity that no doubt was made to fill the void left by *Star Wars,* and to make use of newly invented cheap visual effects. Hopper plays high school science teacher Mr. Roberts, a caring teacher who is partial to a quick natural high and continues to carry some disregard for authority, a hangover from his time as a peace activist during the social revolution of the sixties. Although this is a minor role, Hopper's performance remains memorable. The teenage heroes of *My Sciences Project* discover a piece of alien technology left over from a UFO crash that happened decades earlier. This piece of technology opens a gateway to moments in history, merging time and space. When the teens show Mr. Roberts the device, he gets sucked in to the vortex and disappears for the remainder of the film. The teens are left to fight off dinosaurs, Neolithic ape-men and futuristic monsters, which have descended on their school via the time vortex. At the end of the movie Mr. Roberts returns from a flash of light looking like

Easy Rider's Billy (or *Flashback's* Huey Walker), with shaggy hair, beard and moleskin jacket, preaching revolution and raving about Woodstock and The Beatles.

Although there is no direct referencing of *Easy Rider* in Hopper's third directorial effort, the dark and deeply nihilistic *Out of the Blue* (1980), Hopper does try to inject an edge of similarity between the two films, "You could say that the father and the mother probably saw *Easy Rider* and that the father was probably a biker in his day".[1] Hopper is perhaps suggesting or offering an alternative ending to *Easy Rider's* Billy if he had survived the shooting, which we are led to believe ends his life at the end of *Easy Rider*. Or maybe Hopper is commenting on the direction his own generation headed towards after the social upheaval of the sixties. The audiences that lapped up *Easy Rider's* statement of intent, but neglected to do anything constructive with it are now on the receiving end of *Out of the Blue's* nihilism. The utopianism that *Easy Rider* pointed towards perished in the seventies and eighties, replaced in some cases by heavy drug and drink dependencies, greed and a capitalist delusion.

Most disturbingly during his second renaissance in the eighties Dennis Hopper seriously considered the idea of a sequel to *Easy Rider*. The proposed plotline consisted of a resurrected Billy and Wyatt, blazing across a post apocalyptic dystopian American landscape. How and why this would happen was thankfully never explained. Depending on the proposed films budget and its creative team, one could envision the film as a idiosyncratic take on the post punk scene that had become commonplace in American independent films of the eighties, such as the Alex Cox directed *Repo Man* (1984) and *Straight to Hell* (1987), made for $1,000,000 apiece, or the burning landscape and desolation of the original *Mad Max* (1979), made for $400,000. However there was always a danger that the film would have become as overblown and irrelevant as the $14,000,000 *Mad Max: Beyond Thunder Dome* (1985), or as excessive as the damp squid that was the $175,000,000 Hopper-starring film *Waterworld* (1995).[2] If *Easy Rider Two* had maintained the original films aesthetics of low budget and improvised shooting and dialogue, it might have been a worthwhile sequel that may have made relevant comments on the failure of the post sixties and the slide into corporate greed of the eighties. However, Hopper and Peter Fonda could not settle their creative differences and the sequel to *Easy Rider* was shelved. During the early nineties acting legend Martin Landau's (*North by Northwest, Ed Wood*) production company began working on a proposed sequel which would follow Wyatt and George Hansen's sons as they retraced their father's steps in an effort to find the men responsible for their deaths. As nothing was ever mentioned again, one can assume it didn't make as far as proposal stage. This round of misfires did not stop another group of independent filmmakers producing an unofficial sequel/prequel to *Easy Rider*.

Easy Rider: The Ride Back premiered in 2009 to little fuss or fanfare. Born out of a lawsuit that pitched the newbie filmmakers against the original producers Bob Rafalson and Burt Schneider over rights and use of unused archival material, the film offered a controversial, revisionist back story to the original film. The story delves into the turbulent family history of Peter Fonda's character Wyatt. Following in Wyatt's footsteps is his younger brother Morgan Williams (played by the mysterious Phil Pitzer, a man who could well be a relation of Peter Fonda's) and his journey across-country that takes in the familiar sights of Billy and Wyatt's original journey. Pitzer's character Morgan even wears the same leather threads as his older brother and rides a stars-and-stripes draped motorcycle. Obviously a labour of love for Pitzer (as well as starring, he also co-wrote the screenplay and co-produced; an effort that took him six years) the film appears to abandon the original films intentions. Although the motorcycles are an important and iconic part of *Easy Rider*, bringing the freedom of the road that both characters so desire, they do not define the film as a whole. The bikes are discarded in the jail scene where Wyatt and Billy first meet lawyer George Hansen (Jack Nicholson) and vanish from the screen again as soon as characters arrive in New Orleans to party with escort girls and partake in the Mardi Gras Festival. That's not to say that the original *Easy Rider* doesn't indulge in some 'bike porn' once in a while. With *Easy Rider: The Ride Back* you get the impression that the filmmakers are bike nuts and have basically crafted a film around the lifestyle and rituals of the outlaw motorcyclist, roaring engines, high speeds and hot leather clad girls. By all accounts it seems that only the hardcore biker communities have truly embraced this film, with screenings at motorcycle festivals across America being hugely successful. However it has, at present, yet to find a mainstream distributor or a general audience. As Hopper himself has stated, *Easy Rider* represented more than motorcycles, in his view: "the country was falling apart: the Vietnam War, the Black Panthers... It was a difficult time: there were riots in every city in the United States."[3] For Dennis Hopper *Easy Rider* was much more than a road movie, a buddy movie, a motorcycle movie, a drug movie or a youth movie. It was everything Hopper wanted to say and more about the country he loved and the era it evoked, and in Hopper's opinion, no other movie ever said it better than his.

Published in *Gadfly*, July 2013

Nobody Puts America in the Corner:
Dirty Dancing and the End of Innocence

A cunning and creative YouTube user (who goes by the name kaflickastan) has posted a re-edited film trailer for the 1987 smash hit movie *Dirty Dancing* and painted the film in the nightmarish and film noir-ish colours of a David Lynch directed film. Taking scenes of the film out of their inoffensive context and recasting them into a perverse and lurid thriller that seems to dispense completely with the sweet coming of age drama that *Dirty Dancing* is renowned for being, and replaces it with a sinister tale of obsession, violence and lust. Yet in fact, *Dirty Dancing* shares more with Lynchian themes than would first appear. Lynch's films often concern themselves with the loss of teenage innocence, and the corruption and darkness that lies under the veneer of the American Dream. Lynch's films also deal with the merging of different timeframes, think to Lynch's 1986 film *Blue Velvet*, with its bizarre mixture of the fifties and eighties aesthetics. This is also apparent in *Dirty Dancing's* early sixties setting that merges fragments of the immaculate fifties with the emerging sixties idealism that would soon appear in one of the most culturally seismic decades in history. *Dirty Dancing's* use of popular music on its soundtrack also mixes raunchy sixties dance numbers with staple eighties soft-rock ballads. *Dirty Dancing* is more than a simple story of sweet romance and sexualized dancing. The film explores the loss of innocence, not just with its main characters, but also the loss of innocence that American the sixties would experience as well. If David Lynch had been given the opportunity to direct *Dirty Dancing*, the swearing might have been astronomical, but there would be a possibility that the film would not have turned out all that different.

The character of sixteen-year-old Frances 'Baby' Houseman

(Jennifer Grey) begins the film with aspirations to study economics and join the Peace Corps. Her only true love in life is the love she feels for her caring and encouraging father. The affluent Houseman family, consisting of Baby's mother, her doctor father and her sister Lisa, a wannabe singer, are holidaying for the summer at a resort in the tranquil Catskill Mountains owned by the wealthy Max Kellerman (Jack Weston). That her nickname is Baby, says a great deal about her situation in life. She knows nothing yet of boys, sex or any other vice. The character of Baby is the distillation of the purity and optimistic aspirations of America in 1963, the year in which the film is set. American involvement in the Vietnam War had begun, and although, unlike previous conflicts, news anchors and journalists were there on the front line, sending back gruesome and terrifying reportage, the escalation of the war would not peak until the mid to late-sixties, and there was still optimism that the conflict would be short and with minimum casualties to American troops. Still, the gruesome images would expose Americans to a kind of warfare that they had never witnessed before, and the effects would eventually seep into the American consciousness. The stalemate of the Cold War had seen a heated stand-off the previous year between America and the USSR during the thirteen day Cuban Missile Crisis, yet Mutually Assured Destruction had been avoided by employing diplomacy rather than the taking-up of arms, and thus the long running conflict (1947-1991) would remain relatively tepid. America felt righteous and in control of its own destiny. Yet on the horizon lay the exploration and eventual exploitation of sex, music and drugs that would define the generation of hippies, bikers and drug-induced weirdoes that would soon populate and ultimately define the decade. The rhetoric of the mid to late sixties uttered by counter-culture icon Timothy Leary would be 'turn on, tune in, drop out'[1], a motto that insisted it was time to stop engaging with traditional mainstream society. This shift in social thinking would be triggered by the violent and repeatedly televised assassination of President John F. Kennedy in November 1963; America would never seem so innocent again. Baby's own loss of innocence begins when she is invited to a secret after-hours party that is held by the resorts working class staff of waiters, servants and bartenders. Baby is confronted not only by people with whom she has had no previous experience (i.e. the Working Class), but also the Mambo, a Latin dance originating from Cuba (the act of dancing a Cuban rhythm might possibly be considered treasonous in 1963, a mere one year after the missile crisis). Equally intrigued and intimidated by the resorts lead dancer, the handsome and enigmatic Johnny Castle (Patrick Swayze), she begins to secretly spend time with the resorts staff and learn to dance in their subversive style. From this point Baby seems to open herself up to new experiences and possibilities, yet, for the time being, hides her new-found friends from her straight-laced family.

Baby is later faced with a much more alarming event. She learns that Johnny's dancing partner Penny (Cynthia Rhodes), is pregnant with one of the resorts waiters, the sleazy womanizing Robbie, who also happens to be courting Baby's sister, Lisa (and should be noted is an avid reader of neo-liberalist Ayn Rand). Though not telling her father the real reason, she persuades him to loan her the money in order for Penny to get an abortion (unheard of in 1963, it would still be ten years before the landmark case of *Roe v Wade* implemented a change in law which permitted woman the right to abortion within the first trimester of pregnancy). Baby offers to temporarily take Penny's place as Johnny's dance partner at a performance at another nearby resort. They learn the basic steps and through the music and movement of dancing, Baby begins to explore her own emerging sexuality and her attraction to Johnny. The performance goes well, but on their return, Penny is in agonizing pain due to her botched backstreet abortion. Baby wakes her father and pleads with him to help Penny. He does so, but now knowing what the loan was for, his feelings of betrayal are made clear to Baby and Johnny, whom he believes, though mistakenly, was the father of Penny's aborted child. Baby's father forbids her ever to see Johnny again. Of course, Baby's new found love of dancing and her profound attraction to Johnny means that she will continue to secretly meet with him, even against her father's wishes. In a later scene Baby and her father confront their differences; with Baby accusing her father of having double standards in his aspirations for her future, that in fact her father really wishes that Baby would marry a successful Harvard graduate, from the same social class as her, and have a family of her own. It is clear that Baby's future ambitions, that both she and her father once held, have been replaced with a desire to explore the world on her own terms. From this conversation onward, the nuclear family unit of the Houseman's begins to break apart and may never be the same again. The film ends with a rowdy dance sequence led by Johnny and Baby that momentarily brings the classes and the generations together. Baby's father and Johnny bury the hatchet, and the passing of Baby from father to partner is complete. After this moment ends we can safely assume Baby will explore and even indulge her new found freedom, alongside the rest of her newly unshackled generation.

Baby's end of innocence follows a similar, yet obviously less devastating, trajectory as the teenage characters devised by David Lynch. *Blue Velvet's* Jeffery Beaumont descends into an ugly underworld of drug crime, rape and murder that inhabits the peaceful town of Lumberton. His innocence is lost at the vile hands of the psychotic criminal Frank Booth, who exposes him to a combination of sex, violence and menace. In *Twin Peaks*, the investigation into the death of the beautiful and popular Laura Palmer's reveals a tragic past of abuse and violence at the hands of her own father, who was at the time of the abuse possessed by a malevolent entity. These characters, as well as Baby, begin with idealistic expectations of adulthood, which are destroyed by an unrelenting reality. For Jeffery it is Frank Booth; for Laura it is her abusive father; for Baby it is her sexual attraction to Johnny, the over-nurturing of her father, Penny's abortion and her generation's shift towards a different sort of independence.

It is perhaps a coincidence that Frances's nickname is Baby, she is of the generation of post-war baby boomers who brought about a change in American culture, politics and society. With her intention to study economics and join with the Peace Corps Baby already has the desire to change the world. When she falls for Johnny, her ambitions most likely change, but the generation of which she and her contemporaries are a part would inflict massive changes in social and cultural thinking. Baby's desire to embrace her own independence and break away from family comfort zones and expectations mirrors the generational shift that occurred during the early-to-mid sixties, as more and more young people embraced the freedom of independence and broke from the tradition of the family unit. Although Baby herself and those around her seem unable to identify, let alone articulate, the cultural shift and the decade's loss of innocence that is taking place, the resort owner Max Kellerman, a man of advancing years and in no way hip to the sixties trends, seems to recognize that change happening. In the much celebrated end scene, the resort's staff of waiters and hostesses stand on stage and sing the Kellerman anthem, whilst the working class staff of dancers, bartenders and servants stand, unwanted and unimpressed at the back of the theatre. Kellerman stands in the wings, and while waiting for his solo within the song he states, somewhat bewildered, to Tito, the resort's bandleader: "It all seems to be ending. You think kids want to come with their parents to take foxtrot lessons? Trips to Europe, that's what the kids want. Twenty-two countries in three days. It feels like it's all slipping away". He then joins his staff in the song. Kellerman understands that his own generation's time is up, the righteousness of the American

Dream and family values, held to triumph throughout the depression years, the war years, and the post war years, have slipped away and a new younger generation that is dissatisfied with their forbearers is about to shake society to its very foundations. The kids of the sixties would very soon start to have the time of their lives.

Mumblecore in Obama's America

With every US Presidential Administration a characteristic type
of film genre emerges to help summarize the mood and the
policies that are in effect. From Hollywood the films are typically
pro-American action movies that propagandize internal and
external polices. This level of jingoism reached its zenith in the
1980s with action stars such as Arnold Schwarzenegger,
Sylvester Stallone, and Bruce Willis all starring in films that
depicted positive endorsements of American Foreign Policy (see
Commando, Arnold Schwarzenegger and U.S Foreign Policy). This
form of propaganda was not put to rest by the Bill Clinton,
George W. Bush or Barack Obama administrations, but it was
toned down somewhat. During the Bill Clinton years the
weapons and bloody violence were replaced with savvy liberal
political films such as *Dave* (1993) and *Primary Colours* (1998)
starring John Travolta which painted a picture of a likable, if
flawed, liberal-minded man of the people in the presidential
office to comic and also dramatic effect. During the George W.
Bush administration, jingoism and violence returned with an
added pulling of the heartstrings of the post-9/11 era. Films
directly concerned with 9/11 such as *World Trade Centre* (2006),
the television movie, *Flight 93* (2006), and the high octane *United
93* (2006), allowed audiences to feel that the War on Terror was a
just cause. However, alongside these pro-American features
were the more critical voices found in documentaries such as
Michael Moore's *Fahrenheit 9/11* (2004) and *Sicko* (2007), as well as
geopolitical films such as *Babel* (2006) and *Syriana* (2005), which
answered the "why do they hate us?" question uttered numerous
times by Americans after 9/11. So far Hollywood's answer to the
Barack Obama administration has been to pretend that nothing
is amiss. Over the past four years Hollywood has lambasted the
film market with pure spectacle that, much like the Reagan/Bush

era, has painted America in unreal terms as the greatest and mightiest of nations. Much like American cinema of the late-sixties and early-seventies, in which independent and critical voices arose out of the dying embers of Hollywood's epic productions, it has been up to the young independent filmmakers to capture the era and tell the real story of what it means to be young in Barack Obama's America. This has lead to an emerging sub-genre in independent film that has been given the term Mumblecore by its main proponents.

Mumblecore's history is extremely brief. Emerging during the post 9/11 years, the first film considered Mumblecore was Andrew Bujalski's 2002 film *Funny Ha Ha*. The film's distinct low budget characteristics and naturalistic acting style from its entirely non-professional cast, harked back to the days of New Hollywood filmmaking in the sixties and seventies, and especially the improvised looseness seen in the films of John Cassavetes. The genre progressed with films such as *The Puffy Chair* (2005) and *In Search of a Midnight Kiss* (2008) gaining enthusiastic reviews and film festival awards, but not much in the way of major cinematic screenings. Despite this, the genre's tiny budgets meant that often the filmmakers made an honest return profit from even the smallest of art house screenings, allowing the filmmakers to continue exploring the genre on their own terms. It was from 2008 that Mumblecore started to garner interest from the cinema going public and Hollywood's periphery. Films such as *Humpday* (2009), *Cyrus* (2010), *Tiny Furniture* (2011), *Jeff, Who Lives at Home* (2012) and *Your Sister's Sister* (2012) gained extremely positive reviews from respectable mainstream sources and found audiences beyond their cult standing. It was also during this period of time that some directors of Mumblecore went beyond the genre's amateurish aesthetics and worked with bigger budgets and bigger names. *Cyrus* for example was made with a seven million dollar budget and actors such as Jonah Hill, John C. Riley and Catherine

Keener. The leap was massive when compared with directors Jay and Mark Duplass's 2005 film, *The Puffy Chair*, which had been made for $15,000 and starred mainly their college friends and co-workers. Between *The Puffy Chair* and *Cyrus* the brothers Duplass became superstars of the Mumblecore genre. Mark Duplass became a recognisable face within the genre, not only co-directing and co-writing some of the key works, but also acting in films such as *Hannah Takes the Stairs* (2007), *Humpday* and the Hollywood meets Mumblecore production, *Greenberg* (2010).

The Mumblecore genre mainly focuses on a handful of characters and their, often messy, personal circumstances. Obvious political or social commentary tends to be left off the agenda in most of the films, with perhaps the exception of *Medicine for Melancholy* (2008), which dealt with the lack of African-Americans in San Francisco's apparently 'raceless' hipster culture. The film was timely to say the least, as then Illinois Senator Barack Obama was on the campaign trail to become America's first African-American President. Politics may not be a context, but it certainly is a subtext of Mumblecore's characters and their predicaments. Mumblecore's represented demographic of mostly white middle-class kids provides a snapshot of contemporary middle-class American life. Most of the characters are from liberal backgrounds, sons and daughters of the late baby boomers of the sixties and seventies, often fresh out of college with artistic or literary degrees and returning home to unearth the next stage of their life. A characteristic theme throughout most of films is that of disenchantment with the world and the disillusion of impending adulthood and grown-up responsibility, something that the characters seem ill equipped to handle. The dire economic situation in America and the lack of post-graduate jobs, affordable accommodation and healthcare meant that many independent young people had no choice but to reluctantly return to the family nest. The films of the Mumblecore genre feature characters still living at home beyond their expected time, as is the case with *Jeff, Who Lives at Home* and *Cyrus,* or returning home to reflect on their life after years working or studying away from home, as is the case with the Lena Dunham film *Tiny Furniture* and director Bradley Rust Gray's *The Exploding Girl* (2009). Economic dependency on the parents is a running theme throughout the genre and the characters are in constant search for get-rich-quick or invigorating alternatives to mundane day jobs, which can be seen with the making of the homoerotic-gonzo porn film attempted by two best friends in *Humpday* and the writing of a schlock horror movie by four struggling actors in *Baghead* (2008). When the characters are not living at home they live bohemian lifestyles in cheap and small one-bedroom apartments or shared accommodation with partners or friends.

Like the best social commentary Mumblecore refuses to directly comment on the political and cultural circumstances of its time. By focussing on universal themes of love, jobs, education, friendships, longing, and freedom, the genre subtly explores the life and times of the era. Other era defining books and films from the past have followed this tradition. Jack Kerouac's seminal 1957 book, *On The Road,* which characterized the post-war candor and the freeform jazz of the late fifties, or the 1969 film *Easy Rider,* which rounded up the sixties counterculture of civil rights and civil unrest without directly witnessing those seismic events (see *How Dennis Hopper Conquered the American Century*), or Hunter S. Thompson's 1972 mix of fiction and reportage *Fear and Loathing in Las Vegas,* which explored the souring of the post sixties utopia and the freefall into drugs, greed, madness and paranoia that was the early seventies. In retrospect these three examples subtly commented on the eras in which they were produced, yet at the time, they were perceived as just another part of the changing cultural landscape in art and literature. Mumblecore, in its own subtle way, is defining the present era in American culture. The characters in many of the

Mumblecore productions are at a crossroads in life, embracing or avoiding decisions that will have enormous impact on their future. America is also facing that same crossroads where its own indecision is widespread. The re-election of Barack Obama in 2012 with the merest majority of the popular vote proves that there is much division about the direction the country should take. What is clear from the Mumblecore genre is that it is the young middleclass who are the ones being demolished by the unaccountable capitalism that is rife in America. It is the young liberal-minded, and we should remind ourselves, the future leading citizens of America, who are facing the toughest challenges that economic downturn brings. The films of Mumblecore show a growing apathy and dislocation towards the wider world. Considering Barack Obama's initial presidential campaign ignited young people's interest in politics for the first time in decades, the aftermath of his first four years in power has left many young people deeply discouraged and disenchanted. But with his election win in 2012, there is new opportunity. So, let us anticipate the remainder of his second term will finally bring the 'hope' and 'change' to America that Obama's campaign once promised.

Published in *Scholardarity*, December 2012

Digital Socialism: How Mumblecore Filmmaking is Defying Capitalism

Capitalism has fast-forwarded our manufacture and consumption of popular culture. What might have taken us centuries to make and consume has evolved in the space of fifty to sixty years. Our frenzied desire to acquire shiny new technologies and become part of the latest fads in fashion and culture has meant that we have consumed vast amounts of ideas, objects and information in a very short space of time. Capitalism, by its very nature, is in need of constant expansion, relentlessly creating brand new and alluring markets in order to survive. We seem to have now reached a zenith where no absolutely new form or genre of music, art, fashion or film can be created in any original sense. We can only adapt and reinterpret old ideas to create something that resembles, on the surface at least, an original idea. This has led to subgenre categories in all forms of media, and films in particular have been carved up into subdivisions and then remerged in an attempt to create different genres. However, this does not mean that just because we look to the past for inspiration or to dilute a genre that we use the same creative instruments to reinvent the past. New, cheaper and more accessible film technology has opened a crack in the capitalist system of Hollywood and its subsidiaries that is being pried open further by the auteur filmmakers of the Mumblecore movement.

Mumblecore is defined as a sub-genre of independent filmmaking that relies heavily on low budget production values, and a naturalistic acting style from predominantly non-professional actors. The genre uses realistic, and often impromptu, dialog. Scripts, if used at all, are only loosely adhered to, and an environment of improvisation and cooperation is greatly encouraged. The films are most often shot on digital film and rely heavily on natural light to illuminate the action. Scenes are filmed in the actors' apartments and in real city streets, parks, cafés, nightclubs and bars. The films of the Mumblecore genre are often collaborative productions with actor, videographer, sound recordist and editor all having creative and often financial input in the film's production. The Mumblecore films are mainly distributed via small independent film distribution companies and are features of the indie film festival circuits throughout the world. The films rarely play to mass cinema audiences, but the respectable audience for such independent screenings usually turn a handsome profit on a meagre production cost. For example Mark and Jay Duplass's film *The Puffy Chair* (2005) made $192,467 domestically on a $15,000 production budget. The brothers later, bigger budget production *Cyrus* (2010) made $9,923,855 domestically on a $7 million budget.[1] The content of Mumblecore films may not be original; the filmmakers take their cues from the New Hollywood movement of the late sixties and early seventies, as well as the low budget independent productions of actor and director John Cassavetes. However, unlike the protagonists of New Hollywood who relied on a list of film executive contacts to fund and promote their projects, the filmmakers of the Mumblecore movement require only a small amount of money and a group of willing friends and colleagues to complete their projects.

Mumblecore, and the rise of digital film, is defying the capitalist ideal in two distinct ways. Firstly, with digital film evolving from expensive physical film stock to non-physical data streams, its lack of actual physical existence means its future is not baked in nostalgia, and cannot become victim to the capitalist system and sub-economy of fad film memorabilia that often consists of framed and certified film cells, as well as props and costumes from the within the film's production. The genre also falls well under the radar of fan fairs and memorabilia conventions such as Comic-Con and similar mass moneymaking events.

Although the more corporate film festivals such as Cannes have embraced the genre, the films' first screenings are more suited to small-scale boutique cinemas and art spaces. Mumblecore films made by small production teams are filmed within the context of real life. So instead of props and soundstages that populate large studio productions, auteur productions are filmed in the houses, work places and communal areas of the film's cast and crew, thus dispensing with props and even costumes, as these films also tend to use the cast's own rather ragged looking clothing. To quote Marx and Engel's infamous line from *The Communist Manifesto:* "all that is solid melts into air;"[2] the solidity and physicality of film is evaporating into nothingness. The films themselves that emerge from the genre are the only sellable product of the production; everything else within the film returns to its real life context. Digital film now has a very different future to embrace, which capitalism (by way of its rush to create and sell new technology) has inadvertently laid in front of it.

Secondly, as digital technology has become widely and cheaply available to the masses, it moves further away from the capitalist ideal by undercutting tightly controlled, and previously necessary capitalist processes of distribution. In the past, cameras, film stock, sound recording equipment, editing software and the computers used to process the edits cost a small fortune. Today all this technology is readily available, easy to use and relatively inexpensive. Although the professional sound, audio and editing equipment used by the studios is vastly expensive and still out of reach to most consumers, the cheaper, yet still durable, domestic equipment available, means that any potential filmmaker or documentarian can afford to purchase the technology required to make a quality piece of cinema. Moreover, the internet has opened up the distribution network of independently made films. Small-scale productions can be easily uploaded to video streaming sites and viewed by thousands.

Eventually, the films of Mumblecore could be completely distributed digitally, dispensing with DVD and Blu-ray, and undercutting the capitalist system of current movie distribution. Digital technology has taken the elitism of film away from the studios and placed power in the hands of independent filmmakers and created a more egalitarian method of filmmaking. The Mumblecore movement is a by-product of this access to affordable equipment. There is evidence to suggest that the Mumblecore ethos is being adapted by other filmmakers outside of the United States. The Berlin Mumblecore Movement has produced award-winning films away from the restrictions of the German film industry. The Berlin version of the genre also uses internet crowd funding, websites such as Kickstarter.com and Indigogo.com, to raise small financial funds for the production of the films from like-minded individuals, creating an even more communal experience than its American counter-part.

In my earlier essay *Mumblecore in Obama's America*, I made a case for how Mumblecore is fast becoming the definitive film genre of the Obama-era. The characters that populate the genre are bright, young and liberally educated, yet also on the harsh receiving-end of the current economic downturn that has meant many young people with liberal arts educations returning to the family home for parental support. This reflects the current reality in America. However, from the filmmaker's perspective, Mumblecore is a reaction to the diminishing funding institutions for small and independent films, and the shunning of new and talented filmmakers by the mainstream Hollywood production houses. A rising trend throughout the last five years in most business sectors has been to hire interns, who remain unpaid and partake in the thankless and mundane day-to-day tasks and then are dispensed with, to be replaced by another troop of disposable and desperate hopefuls. This has led to a mainstream system that is in absolute lockdown. An outsider cannot penetrate it without serious economic self-sacrifice. The filmmakers of the

Mumblecore genre, who come from working-to-middle class backgrounds, have concluded that creating a film as part of its own economic support network is a cheaper and far more creatively rewarding option than a brief and unpaid internship with a studio. In this sense, Mumblecore is creating its own self-sustaining system alongside the mainstream.

One cannot ignore that over the last few decades the cult of the producer and director in mainstream films has created a deeply unequal and egotistical environment in filmmaking. Capitalism has allowed the creative industry to pull focus on the individual and the entitlements they deem to warrant. Mumblecore dispenses with the cult of personality that surrounds most contemporary producers and directors and allows for a collective and equal participation in all the stages of film production, something virtually unheard of within Hollywood circles. The genre's productions are open, innovative, improvisational and egalitarian. This collectivism of creativity is producing truthful depictions of life in America for a miniscule budget. This socialism of filmmaking, from the inexpensive equipment to the ethics of production, may be mainstream cinema's saving grace. After all it was New Hollywood's reduced budgets, guerrilla-style filmmaking and savvy knowledge of youth culture that saved the studios of the sixties and seventies when they too were pouring millions into star-studded and inoffensive big screen spectacles. Hollywood today is repeating history with grossly excessive budgets being spent on an endless barrage of mindless nonsense. Mumblecore is following New Hollywood's path and is telling stories about what life is really like in America and the world. If Hollywood can be brave like it once was and entrust a small budget to a talented production group, then it could be, for the film world, small-scale socialism that saves capitalism.

Published in *Scholardarity*, March 2013

North Korea in Fiction and as Fiction

According to the remake of *Red Dawn* (2012) the communist threat is back. At the peak of the Cold War the original *Red Dawn*, released in 1984 and starring soon to be megastars Patrick Swayze and Charlie Sheen, showed a rag-tag army of teenagers take on the might of an invading Soviet Red Army. The new *Red Dawn* follows the same narrative, except this time around the invading force is North Korea, the isolated East Asian communist state. Whereas in the mid-eighties the prospect of a Russian-led assault on American soil was reasonable to imagine, North Korea poses no similar threat. At present the country is in economic turmoil, and led by the incredibly young and untested Kim Jong-Un along with a squabbling gang of military elders. North Korea's army, although numbering over a million troops, is undernourished by years of cripplingly bad crop harvests whilst its antiquated military equipment harks back to the once glorious days of the 1970s when the Soviet Union was its key sponsor and provider of arms. As much as North Korea postures about its place in the world and flaunts its nuclear program, it also pouts and whimpers over its hardships, and is in constant need of aid and economic assistance from China, its only real ally. Unlike in the eighties, where American government administrations and Hollywood painted the Russians as the clear-cut bad guys, today the enemy is less clear. The War on Terror has meant that instead of being at war with a nation, America and its allies are engaged in an unpopular war with an ideal, and ideals are notoriously difficult to portray as deadly or malevolent on film. Thus, Hollywood has returned to the Red Threat.

An Asian is an Asian and a Communist is a Communist

Red Dawn was kept out of movie theatres for a number of years due to some postproduction tweaks. The original invading army in the film was communist China. The studio, MGM, reconsidered this move when they thought that communist China would censor the film and lock it out of the lucrative Chinese film market. With some clever edits and use of CGI the foes of *Red Dawn* were changed to communist North Koreans without any re-casting of the antagonist roles; after all, in Hollywood, what is the difference, right? It would seem, in re-making *Red Dawn,* Hollywood has exposed a casual racism and relative unease around foreigners; that it can change a few flags, touch up some dialogue, and suddenly they have a different, yet still deadly communist enemy marching through its film. Interestingly this same scenario was played out a year before *Red Dawn* was released in the video game *Homefront* (2011). In an imaginative prologue, written by *Apocalypse Now* and original *Red Dawn* screenwriter John Milius, a unified Korea has become a major global power under the leadership of Kim Jong-Un, the son of Kim Jong-Il. The demise of the American empire and an Asian Bird Flu epidemic has left the United States extremely vulnerable. The Koreans launch an attack that leads to the occupation of much of the US Pacific Coast, thus the fight to re-take America begins. The original enemy in *Homefront* was intended to be Chinese, until game developers thought better of it. In an article entitled *China Is Both Too Scary and Not Scary Enough To Be Video Game Villains,* the games publisher Danny Billson from THQ commented "China is like America's factory. Everything you buy is made in China."[1] This comment is right, if slightly narrow in perspective. China is often regarded as the world's factory, not just America's. The title of the article perhaps tells us more about America's tepid relationship with China. The prospect of an invasion by Chinese forces would hardly seem likely in the current globalized environment, yet the fear is that should it happen America would be almost powerless to withstand it, judging by the economic and militaristic might of

China and its ever growing global support network. China's merging of traditional communism and modern free market capitalism has boosted the country's economic growth beyond any speculator's wildest dreams, rigorously catching up with America. China no longer has any legitimacy as a communist threat due to its embrace of free-market capitalism; essentially, its reliance on production is just as important as the world's reliance on its produce. China is too scary a prospect to antagonize, yet its seemingly undeviating place in the world fosters a sense of the ordinary which makes it not scary enough.

The Fictional State

It is perhaps easy for Hollywood to portray North Korea as a fictional enemy when so much of North Korea's actual history and culture has been fictionalized by its very own leadership. Kim Jong-un, the young and portly current leader is the third in a dynastic line of Kims to lead the country under the ideology of Juche (loosely translated to mean self-reliance) and to maintain a hard-line and xenophobic attitude to other countries and other political ideologies. His father, the late Kim Jong-Il, was perhaps the most prolific author of much of North Korea's recent fictional history. His own father Kim Il-Sung led the country out of the Korean War and into its first decades of early prosperity and it was Kim Il-Sung who adapted Stalinist and Confucian thinking to his own Juche ideology. It was the son Kim Jong-Il who propelled the cult of personality that surrounded them both into the homes and lives of the North Korean people, via the strong use of social-realist propaganda and state owned media, which pumps anti-Western sentiment to the masses and proposes that the country needs nothing and has nothing to envy of the rest of the world. In the book *The Cleanest Race* (2010) by B.R. Myers, the propaganda and deeply xenophobic outlook of the North Koreans is explored in great depth. The God-like graphic depictions, which are not photographs, show Kim Il-Sung or Kim Jong-Il dispensing on the spot advice to the Korean workers, or embracing their comrades to demonstrate a leadership that is, and has always been, concerned for its citizen's welfare. The Kim dynasty has developed this propaganda to fool its own people into believing this fictional history. It is perhaps not surprising that Kim Jong-Il was an author of many books on the artistic and political development of film and literature. Known to write and direct both films and operas in his early years, Kim Jong-Il would have been suited to, and even perhaps would have preferred, an artistic life. Instead public duties called when he was named heir apparent to his father in the mid 1970s. His new role and ever increasing responsibilities within the political institutions did not impede him dictating his theories of cinema and literature. His books *On the Art of Cinema* (2001) and *On the Art of Opera* (2001) feature doctrine on story and characters, narrative and exposition. These books, combined with numerous other works, create an internal machine that peddles North Korea's alternative narrative and its dogmatic socialist view to its own citizens, and in effect, lays the foundation for a fictional state that its author has implemented, not in film, but in the everyday. Whole sections of *On the Art of Cinema* are devoted to laying waste to Hollywood style filmmaking:

> In the capitalist system of film-making the director is called "director", but, in fact, the right of supervision and control over film production is entirely in the hands of the tycoons of the film-making industry who have the money, whereas the directors are nothing but their agents[2]

A valid point, especially when you take into account the changes made to *Red Dawn*. In a way, North Korea resembles a cinematic caricature of a communist state, dreamt up by Hollywood to be the industry standard for corruption and evil; a point that is lampooned with hysterical results in *Team America: World Police* (2004). The tragedy is that North Korea is very real, and its corruption of its own citizens is even more a terrible reality.

Happy to be bad

One cannot help but think that every time North Korea is pushed into the antagonist's role its leadership rejoices. The country's leadership has been trying for decades to portray itself to the outside world as a formidable beast that retains unaccountability for its actions; Hollywood is perhaps better equipped for the job than the leadership of North Korea. The country's nuclear program is a subject of much speculation, and recently became a very concerning predicament for the world, with North Korean rhetoric against South Korea becoming more bloodthirsty than its usual fiery posture. Some believed it to be a real threat, whilst others regard it as a blackmail tool to obtain more aid assistance. Either way, it has worked. America is in a constant game of cat and mouse as it tries to broker deals with the regime to break off its nuclear program and participate in diplomacy; which it usually does for a while at least until it feels that it is losing face, and then reinstates the program and takes antagonistic action, like the recent rocket launch and shelling of Yeonpyeong, a disputed South Korean island. These actions raise opposition voices from most of the world's nations, but very little action has been taken, apart from economic sanctions, which ultimately punish the people of North Korea far more than the leadership. The reality is that the North Korean leadership is not the formidable beast it wishes it could be, but a whimpering wounded animal left to wander in the wastelands of the Cold War, still snapping and bearing its teeth at anything that comes to close, but should the need arise, quick and easy to slay from afar. However that being said, the North, in its initial defence could inflict a massive amount of damage to the region. In the future we will no doubt see North Korea return to the antagonist role in popular culture, the country, put simply, is too weird and too scary to ignore.

Published in *The Fear of Monkeys*, February 2013

How to Make a Film in North Korea...
If you had to

However much a government interferes with the lives of its population it seems to never try to dictate the expression of art to its creative citizens. Over the centuries and throughout the world, art has been the one medium in which people could express their concerns, hopes and dreams without political intrusion. The early and mid twentieth century created a small blip, with their wars and political posturing oppressive governments used the emerging medium and technology of film to instigate government controlled art and film propaganda in order to construct notions of statehood and patriotism in a time of conflict. The most apparent examples were the socialist realism that emerged from the former Soviet Union and its sphere of influence, and, of course, Hitler's Germany. At present when governments try to interfere with the production of films within their own country they are target of bitter criticism by the artistic community. For example in 2011 British Prime Minister David Cameron suggested that the UK film industry produce more 'commercial' and 'rewarding' films in the same vein as *The Queen* (2006) or *The Kings Speech* (2010) that could turn a profit and also promote a grand appearance of The United Kingdom to the world.[1] The backlash came from far and wide with British filmmakers such as Ridley Scott and Hollywood veteran Robert Redford denouncing Cameron's narrow and capitalist view of artistic expression. In most modern societies artistic expression is required to be isolated from the establishment so that it can freely comment, analyze and criticize it. There is however still one place left in the world that dictates the production of art and film, that place is North Korea. North Korea's leadership has for decades put the needs of its own social revolution and outward appearance before that of individual artistic endeavour. This has meant that the film and artistic output of North Korea directly corresponds with the leadership's outdated socialist ideology that it peddles to its citizens and to the world.

To understand the restrictive nature of filmmaking and art in North Korea, we must first understand the ideology that informs the nation. Every aspect of daily life in North Korea is to serve the leadership and the country's own official Juche ideology. A rudimentary version of the Juche ideology was created in the late fifties and early sixties at a time when North Korea's economic and social structure was fairly strong, at least compared to its southern neighbour. The Party Leadership required an ideology similar in socialist values to that of Marxism, Stalinism and Maoism, as the country was founded on the military assistance of both Chairman Mao and Stalin. The Juche ideology is credited to the country's eternal president Kim Il-Sung, however it was his son Kim Jong-Il that pulled the loose threads of the ideology together and adapted the theory to all aspects of life and living conditions. In the early seventies Juche became the official doctrine of the county, replacing any remains of the communist-isms. To an outsider of North Korea (and some might argue even an insider) the Juche ideology is virtually impenetrable. Reading any North Korean communiqué is comparable to being bludgeoned over the head with a mighty hammer and sickle. The basic premise from the Juche ideology is this:

The people must have independence in thought and politics, economic self-sufficiency, and self-reliance in defence.

Policy must reflect the will and aspirations of the masses and employ them fully in revolution and construction.

Methods of revolution and construction must be suitable to the situation of the country.

The most important work of revolution and construction is moulding people ideologically as communists and mobilizing them to constructive action.[2]

These four points are in terrible contradiction to the reality of North Korea today, where no freedom in political thought exists and where policy certainly does not reflect the "will and aspirations" of the masses, where internal policy, that serves to maintain the power of the leading elite, has crippled the economy and left a large majority the population starving, homeless and reliant on food and medical aid from NGOs.

Hypothetically speaking making a film in North Korea would be equally a frustrating and liberating prospect. The Juche doctrine on filmmaking that Kim Jong-Il authored in 1987 titled *The Cinema and Directing* is a manifesto for filmmakers that deeply imbeds the ideology into every aspect of the creative process with militant use of language. The first chapter of the book: 'The Director is the Commander of the Creative Group' sets the tone. The idea proposed in this chapter is that the director holds the creative vision and flair, but cannot accomplish his vision without the creative group, therefore the production team becomes akin to a military unit, working together in harmony and equality with each other. It is somewhat refreshing to read praise for the lowest production member who goes unnoticed in so many mainstream Western productions: "Since the film is made through the joint efforts and wisdom of many people, every participant in the production should fulfill their role and responsibility like the master he is."[3] By comparison, in the Hollywood system the use of solidarity and comradeship is nonexistent in the age of egotistical and dictatorial directors such as *Titanic* and *Avatar* director James Cameron. In fact the egotists of Hollywood could learn something from this manifesto about sharing and exploring their creative vision with others:

In analyzing and considering a production the director should not be too egotistical. Every artist has his own creative individuality and may have different views on a production. If the director does not take this into account and holds his own views and ignores the opinions of other creative workers, it will be difficult to establish a uniform view on a production.

The strength of the new system lies in the fact that it guarantees the solid unity and cohesion of the creative group based on the Juche idea and gives full play to the awareness and credibility of all the members and the director's guidance goes deep into the creative work and life so as to bring about an uninterrupted flow of innovation[4]

The text appears to offer incredible creative freedom for the production group, from the director to the key grip there is a sense of artistic duty to perform, but in reality this is an illusion. All of North Korea's film output is designed solely as propaganda that glorifies the leadership, the nation and the doctrine of Juche. No film or art can criticize or comment negatively on the hardships faced by the North Korean people throughout the past decades nor condemn the military or leadership. All film production must adhere to the Juche ideology and, as point four above clearly states, must mould its viewers ideologically as communists.

The basic duty of the creative group is to make revolutionary films of high ideological and artistic value, which make an effective contribution to arming people fully with the Party's monolithic ideology[5]

In other words nothing contained within the film can go off message from the Party line.

The ideological kernel of a production is the seed which the director and all the other creative workers should bring into flower through their collective efforts and wisdom... Therefore, the director should be very careful that none of the creative team loses the seed or introduces anything which has nothing to do with it.[6]

One only assumes that the 'seed' to which Kim Jong-Il is encouraging the film crew to bring to flower is the Juche ideology itself.

There are many admirable aspects of *The Cinema and Directing*. It would appear that Kim Jong-Il would have perhaps been more comfortable in the director's chair as opposed to the dictators' throne. Without the nonsensical Juche popping up in virtually every paragraph, and the constant reminders that the film is for revolutionary purposes, the text almost serves as an ideal and practical film production manual. Certainly the aspect of comradeship and equality within the production unit is in itself revolutionary. Mainstream film production systems throughout the world, but especially in Hollywood, rely on the artistic vision and execution of the director. In North Korea the director is simply the leader of the unit and the film production is a collective endeavour.

Despite the recent outward nuclear threat, there might be evidence to suggest that the new leadership in North Korea is at least loosening its grip on the arts or allowing outside influence to modernize the dated narratives of so many North Korean Films. In 2012 a joint British-Belgian-North Korean production titled *Comrade Kim Goes Flying* premiered at the Toronto Film Festival. The film follows the exploits of a young girl as she attempts to leave her mundane life as a coalminer and work in the circus as a trapeze artist. The film is certainly at odds with past North Korean films in that it features a strong female protagonist, a first for North Korean cinema, and is in effect a romantic comedy. The doctrine of Kim Jong-Il's *The Cinema and Directing* is not at all apparent, nor is the current leadership's reestablishment of the Juche ideology (although it does paint life in North Korea in an extremely positive light). *Comrade Kim Goes Flying* may not change the situation in North Korea, but it points to a future in which art can be free from governmental control and fall into the hands of the people. When it eventually does, the freedom of expression that will follow will be hard to suppress.

Published in *Gadfly*, July 2013

Reimagining *Star Trek: The Motion Picture*

Star Trek: The Motion Picture (1979) was the highly criticized, and often ignored, Science Fiction film that initiated a new chapter in the *Star Trek* franchise. It is renowned for its dull and plodding narrative, and for stripping the verve and vigour out of its long serving characters. Despite the fact that two years previously *Star Wars* (1977) had made space an exciting and adventurous place to roam, *Star Trek: The Motion Picture* was literally a galaxy far, far away from the swashbuckling heroics of Luke Skywalker, Han Solo and their attempts to bring down the evil intergalactic Empire. It wasn't always like this. A step back to the late sixties, and the troublesome trio of Captain Kirk, Spock and Doctor McCoy ruled the space lanes and left a galactic trail of fist fights, flaming ships, broken hearts and sarcastic quips. With the return of *Star Trek: The Motion Picture*, a more sober, older and wiser crew boarded the Starship Enterprise; and instead of threats from the staple *Star Trek* villains such as the Romulans or Klingons, this voyage was an existential journey that aesthetically had more in common with Stanley Kubrick's *2001: A Space Odyssey* (1968).

The wafer thin premise is this: a monolithic vessel surrounded by dense clouds is on an intercept course to Earth. In its wake, it leaves a path of destruction, and with its intentions unknown, Starfleet command send the freshly built Enterprise to try and engage the phenomenon. The Enterprise crew discovers that at the centre of the vessel is a Voyager 6 Earth probe that has, over the centuries, become sentient and received countless upgrades from unknown aliens. Voyager's (now referred to as V'ger) mission is to return all the data it has gathered to its creator, mankind.

What is striking about *Star Trek: The Motion Picture* is that its apparent lack of action and driving narrative creates a hidden subtext that suggests an emotional attachment or strong sexual arousal towards machinery. As strange as this might sound the film is full of what can only be described as spaceship and technology pornography. Slow crawling pan shots of the Enterprise exterior and close-ups of the Enterprise's bulkheads and engines are accompanied by rousing orchestral music. At one point whilst the ship is cradled in space dock, a dozen tiny figures hover over the ship in white spacesuits making last minute repairs to the immense hull. The scene is meant to illustrate how enormous and overbearing the vessel is, and this obviously works, but one can't help draw inferences to images of microscopic male sperm trying to infiltrate the female egg. This scene of a soft-core money shot of the Enterprise is intercut with Captain Kirk and engineer Scotty approaching in a space shuttle to rendezvous with the Enterprise. Both men look equally nervous and excited, akin to how two peeping schoolboys might react as they catch their first sight of female breasts through a keyhole. The two men twitch and shuffle, offering each other knowing glances and toothy smiles. The object of their excitement is not female however, but a sexless machine, a concise and flawless construction of cylinders and wires, bulkheads and facets. Although the Enterprise is always referred to as a 'she' by its crew, the ship is anything but female. It is in fact a personalized male play toy. The Enterprise is the ultimate extension of the male appendage: the Porsche or Ferrari of the space age.

Away from the sexualisation of the vessel, the character of navigation officer Ilia throws up a man/machine sexual dilemma, which ultimately becomes the catalyst of the movie. She joins the ship at space dock to the excitement of the crew members and, in particular, handsome First Officer Willard Decker, a former love interest of Ilia. Ilia is a member of the Deltan species, a highly exotic and sexually open society. Deltans emit potent pheromones which provoke strong sexual attraction in other species. When she boards the ship, she announces to Kirk and the bridge crew that her vow of celibacy has been put on record, which, one assumes is some sort of Deltan cultural requirement in order to serve aboard a Starfleet vessel. Although still clearly attracted to one another, Ilia and Decker remain professional, that is, until a probe from V'ger invades the Enterprise and abducts Ilia. When she reappears, she is in fact not Ilia, but an android recreation, sent to record and observe the Enterprise crew and learn of their intentions. She has been stripped of her emotions (and her clothing) and is nothing more than a machine within; even her voice has been distorted to emit a hard clipped tone. Although having none of Ilia's memories or experiences, the android Ilia somehow retains its base feelings towards Decker, and he too is still physically attracted to the android representation of Ilia, although it shares no personality traits with its former incarnation. When the Enterprise transverses the cloud that surrounds the massive ship, they see that at its centre is the space probe Voyager 6, a reconnaissance probe launched from Earth hundreds of years previously. In response to V'ger's intention to merge with its creator, Decker offers himself as the human element that will complete V'gers desire and save Earth from the destructive force of the cloud. He joins with Ilia; they kiss, and a shock of white light merges their bodies into a new life force that vanishes from sight. This appears to be the ultimate convergence of machine and man, both consenting, to join harmoniously.

Despite its dour tone and plodding narrative, *Star Trek: The Motion Picture* began a re-emergence of interest in all things *Star Trek*. The subsequent decades saw the release of eleven further films, joined recently by the J.J. Abrams high octane re-boot *Star Trek* (2009) and *Star Trek: Into Darkness* (2013), and the launch of four long-running and successful television spin-offs including *Star Trek: The Next Generation* (1987-1994). The subtext that emerges in *The Motion Picture* is explored to great lengths in *TNG* by the character of Lieutenant Commander Data, an android with a Pinocchio complex, who wishes to explore human emotions and relationships. It only took till episode three of the first season of *TNG* for the dilemma of man and machine to emerge. In *The Naked Now* (broadcast 5 October 1987) the crew of the new Enterprise are infected with a strange pathogen that eliminates their inhibitions. This pathogen also affects Lieutenant Commander Data. He is seduced by Lieutenant Tasha Yar, the ship's security officer, who asks the forward question of whether he is "fully functional," to which he replies that he is "programmed in multiple techniques, a broad variety of pleasuring", ultimately leading them to engage in sexual intercourse. Data's desire to become human begins with wanting to partake in sexual interaction, as if this is the ultimate step in realizing his goals (becoming a man). Data and V'ger share a similar goal of becoming something more than the sum of their mechanical parts; they desire humanity, which they believe will be attained through sexual or emotional engagement, a trait that has been programmed into their matrix by humans and adapted by the machine.

The Next Generation also introduced *Star Trek's* most deadly enemy The Borg, a species that rather than reproduce, conquers and assimilates other species into its collective by injecting nanoprobes (microscopic robots) into the bloodstream of its victims. These nanoprobes change the genetic structure of the victim, allowing machinery to be implanted inside and upon the body and to replace arms and legs with mechanical limbs. Perhaps in a futile attempt to breathe new life into *Star Trek: The Motion Picture,* a Borg origin story was alluded to in the extras of the DVD release of the movie and the same theory has been added to *The Star Trek Encyclopaedia*. In the film, V'ger is conceived has having been adapted by a species of living machines from a planet an incredible distance from Earth. These living machines are presumed to be an early incarnation, or possibly a sub-species of The Borg. The Borg are living bondage, mindless automatons subservient to a Borg Queen, even their attire resembles a gimp outfit: tight restrictive leather suits, mouths and their eyes covered or sealed shut. When we first meet The Borg Queen in *Star Trek: First Contact* (1996) it soon becomes obvious that her role is that of a dominatrix: she is the mistress to her subordinates and oozes a hypnotic sex appeal.

The exploration of the relationship between man and machine in *Star Trek* throws up an interesting conundrum. Whilst the crews of various Enterprises strive to pursue and embrace technology and emotionally connect with machines by programming rudimentary emotive longing into their matrix, machines unstintingly strive to be more human or seek a form of humanity that their programming lacks, by forming sexual or emotional connections with people. In a sense, the Enterprise crews have inadvertently programmed their own enslavement to machines by expecting so much fulfilment and instant gratification from them. In *Star Trek*, we see machines sexualizing mankind, a role reversal if you will, in which the exploited becomes the exploiter. Our own very real sexualization of technology has already begun in the way the latest gadgets are advertised and presented to us. By preaching to consumer's sense of vanity, they encourage desire of the newest, shiniest and slickest technology available, and sexualized imagery sells these objects in an efficient way. Sex with mechanical instruments, such as vibrators and masturbation machines, has been well established since the sexual revolution of the early 1960s. However, more recent sexual devices have become much more complex, and certainly more mechanical and monstrous looking; leading one to conclude that the next stage in this progression is to follow the path to which *Star Trek: The Motion Picture* has hinted. This leads us to presume that in our own future, as technology develops, we may enter into a disturbing and terrible relationship with machines in which mankind endeavours to become equal on an emotional level with them, whilst machines, in turn, view us as sexual conquests in order to achieve humanity. *Star Trek: The Motion Picture* may one day be seen as prophetic.

Published in *Gadfly*, December 2012

Disaster Movies and the Collective Longing for Annihilation

The majority of the human species breathed a sigh of relief as they woke up Saturday morning December 22nd 2012 to find themselves still among the living and that the world had not ended. The ancient Mesoamerican Long Count calendar, used by the Mayans, among others, and which ended on December 21st, was thought by some to be a prediction of an almighty apocalypse that would leave the world in ruins with only pockets of survivors left. Despite no solid evidence that the Mayans thought the world would end on this date, or that any obvious sign of our destruction was imminent, a niggling doubt floated around in most people's minds. On top of this, religious zealots and conspiracy theorists capitalized on this fear by inventing ludicrous ideas about the Earth's destruction, envisioning a lost planet of our solar system called Nibiru suddenly emerging into our orbit and causing a chain of catastrophic seismic events and eventual collision. Of course natural disasters are nothing to take for granted, as recent events in Japan, New Zealand and Haiti have shown. But doomsayers took these tragic events out of the real devastation they caused and placed them within their own fictional contexts in an attempt to scrape up evidence, thus the freakish amount of earthquakes the world has endured recently was apparently down to gravitational strain from an approaching planet that was shifting the Earth's poles (A Google search of 'Nibiru and earthquakes' brings up many sources for this theory). A minority of the population of earth were left bitterly disappointed that the world had not succumbed to a horrific death and one cannot help but think that producers in Hollywood's biggest studios were among the most disappointed; after all they have been trashing the world to bits on film with all manner of objects and alien entities for decades.

Any predicted end date that history throws up has been exploited by Hollywood. With pre-millennium tension building at the end of the 1990s an assortment of catastrophes were lined up for our entertainment, from fears of gigantic comet bombardment in *Armageddon* (1997) and *Deep Impact* (1997), sinister alien invasion in *Independence Day* (1996) and unstoppable natural disasters in *Twister* (1996) and *Dante's Peak* (1997). The mid-to-late-nineties were fit for a range of disaster movies that had a catch-all quality in the chosen object of destruction. Audiences lapped up these showcases of obliteration and absorbed themselves in the scenes that brought the most mayhem. In films such as *Deep Impact* and *Armageddon*, the real end of the world scenario is avoided by mankind's cunningness. In both films a team is sent to intercept the incoming comet and deposit a nuclear payload to shatter the huge rock into more manageable debris. In *Deep Impact* it doesn't quite go to plan and a mile wide fragment smashes into the Atlantic Ocean that sends a mega tsunami racing in all directions killing millions. The other larger fragment is despatched by the astronauts guiding their damaged ship into a deep crevice and blowing up the comet, and themselves, up from the inside. The scenario in *Armageddon* is the virtually the same, except the impending comet is the size of Texas (696,200 km) and is prefaced by a swarm of smaller meteorites that impact in New York and Paris. NASA sends a rogue team of professional oil drillers, lead by Bruce Willis, to drill down and deposit the bomb and split the comet in two, sending the two large fragments skimming past Earth. The plan works, but only at the very last minute and with the sacrifice of Willis and some of his crew. The Roland Emmerich directed *Independence Day* (1996) laid waste to most of mankind's greatest architectural achievements. Enormous alien vessels hover over every major city in the world and when they finally attack they unleash a mighty death ray that incinerates everything in its path. The scenes of the White House and the Empire State

Building being obliterated were used in the trailer and advertisement spots to whet audiences' appetite for destruction.

After the events of September 11 2001, disaster movies took on an almost prophetic role. The fictional bombardment of America's iconic buildings in Hollywood movies was all too similar to the reality of hijacked passenger planes being flown deliberately into the World Trade Center and the Pentagon. This time the horror was very real. For the time being at least audiences were not comfortable with external threats to their country and their freedoms, when a real, yet seemingly hidden, threat existed somewhere in the world. So as an alternative to external intimidation, Hollywood focused on internal and many would argue man-made threats, the environment and climate change. In *The Day After Tomorrow* (2004), the whole of the northern hemisphere is treated to a onslaught of extreme weather and a series of hurricane style super storms that surge an enormous tidal wave over Manhattan. The temperatures then dramatically plummet freezing the water that has drowned the city. The aftermath of this shows the northern hemisphere completely covered in snow and ice, yet the positive effect seems to be a renewed and clean atmosphere that the storms have created. Although director Roland Emmerich (him again) forgoes scientific fact for movie spectacle, the scenes of destruction at the hands of Mother Nature, something we are powerless to withstand, tap into a collective desire to see mankind and its achievements bite the dust.

With the 2012 Mayan prediction looming, the time was again right for Hollywood to exploit the fear of annihilation. The film *Knowing* (2009) tied together many prophecies, religious conspiracies, and recent natural disasters to conclude that the world would end by a destructive solar flare. The last three minutes of the film show a wall of fire tearing across the Earth and the sky ablaze: all life extinguished. Though poorly executed, M. Night Shyamalan's *The Happening* (2010) had an interesting premise where mankind's destruction is at the hands of plants and trees releasing a defensive toxic vapour, causing humans to kill themselves, as protection from human-produced carbon. External attacks were also back in vogue, with alien invasions happening in *Skyline* (2010), *Battle: LA* (2010) and *Battleship* (2012). However it was down to king of destruction, Roland Emmerich, to give the world an almighty thrashing in the ludicrous yet entertaining *2012* (2010). A cataclysm of events that include polar and continental plate shifts, solar flares, earthquakes, tsunamis and volcanic eruptions, offers the most concise destruction of the planet Earth ever put to film. Again, as with most of Emmerich's movies, science is thrown out in favour of pure spectacle.

Alongside the mainstream disaster movies that have scored with the masses, independent film has also taken the end of the world cues, and dealt with the more existential fears that the Hollywood films have no time for. As the end of the century loomed, the small Canadian film *Last Night* (1998) chronicled the experiences of a group of people in what is literally the last night on earth. In *Last Night* the cause of the extinction event is never revealed, but many see it as a last chance to make human connections on an emotional and physical level. The perhaps Nibiru-inspired small-budget film, *Another Earth* (2011), and the Lars Von Trier directed *Melancholia* (2011), deal with the discovery and approach of a planet in our solar system, and the consequences of that discovery on individuals, not society as a whole. In *Another Earth* the discovery of a twin planet Earth offers hope and a second chance to a young girl who was the instigator of a fatal car accident that killed a man's pregnant wife and child. Although not a disaster movie as such (unless you count the personal devastation of the main character), the film, nevertheless, tapped into the fear of impending and unknown doom from above. In *Melancholia,* the arrival of a planet on a collision course with Earth brings perspective to the lives of a group of wealthy friends and lovers. Whilst Hollywood dazzles us with epic effects, it has been the role of independent film to show the humanistic side of the end of the world scenario. The prospect of annihilation for the characters that populate these films is inevitable and unavoidable, and survival is the last thing on their minds.

It is perhaps Hollywood's compulsive obsession for film-based destruction that has fed mankind's own desire for near-annihilation. I say near-annihilation because there are always survivors who inherit a devastated planet, but have a chance to begin the human race again. In most of Hollywood's disaster movies mankind is offered a fresh start, a chance to rid itself of its vile nature and enter into a utopia of peace and calm. The world is reborn fresh and new after the devastation. Petty divisions in religion, race and nationhood seem to be abolished in favour of human kindred and the greater good. The beliefs in capital wealth and possessions are abandoned and a new respect for nature and mortality are nurtured. Disaster movies encourage our own longing for a better and more equal world. The new world in which we rid ourselves of the shackles of conflicts, belongings and our own emotional baggage, and create a peaceful and serene world that is created on our own terms. Because what we really see in disaster movies, after the destruction, is a chance to try again.

Published in *Gadfly*, March 2013

Louder than War: Have Movies Fallen into the same Loudness Trap as Music?

Over the past few decades modern music has become victim to the age of digital audio production and manipulation. Authentic sounds and instrumentation have been swallowed up by a polished gleam that renders the audio to a glossy and punchy finish. Loudness has been the key to creating upfront and vibrant songs that at first sound exciting. By pitching the quieter moments within an audio track to a higher frequency, the song automatically becomes more urgent and distinctive. This slow change, orchestrated by producers and record companies, has been deliberately subtle, as if to allow listeners ears to adapt to the change in audio quality. This tampering in sound has had an unfortunate drawback for the listener. As producers up the volume within the audio track, listeners have had to reduce their own volume controls to a more comfortable volume, thus the songs initial spark and bluster is reduced to a whimper. This has led to a backlash from music fans who have become frustrated with their favourite artists manipulating their recorded sound. The most documented example of this was Metallica's 2008 album *Death Magnetic* which was released as a CD version with dynamic range compression added (which pushes audio peaks beyond the point of digital clipping, causing distortion) and as a download and playable version on the popular video game *Guitar Hero III*, minus the compression. Fans noticed a distinct clipping sound throughout the CD album, which prompted calls for a re-master of the original recordings to bring them to the same standard as the *Guitar Hero* version.[1] With music, re-mastering and re-editing can at least be done to a reasonable standard. In film, excessive use of special effects, bad dialogue delivery and deafening soundtracks are harder to expel from a film, in fact they are more than likely added on purpose. Film is suffering its own Loudness War that strips away the authenticity, emotional and humanistic elements and instead replaces them with layers of digital spectacle. Once the audience chose heart rendering emotional substance, but film is turning its back on the emotional aspect and looking to dazzle and confuse its audience with simplistic narratives, told with complex digital technology that only engages the sensory level.

There has been much criticism aimed towards music production and the studio trickery employed to produce modern music. Auto-Tune, which digitally tampers with a vocal track to put it in tune, is basically a cheaters program for any potential singer. The criticism mainly takes a swipe at the lack of authenticity that digital audio manipulation permits. Enhancing a singer's vocals or upping the volume of a song in order to give it more of a kick seems to strip it of its original substance. Film on the other hand is often lauded for incorporating similar computer generated cheats that can spawn entire digital landscapes and impossible feats of the imagination. James Cameron's film *Avatar* (2009) may have been criticized for its relatively light-weight story, yet it still dazzled its enormous world-wide audiences with the magical digitally created world of Pandora and its alien inhabitants. *Avatar* is an extreme example of the stripping away of humanity in film and their replacement with digital layers. The film's human actors were recorded delivering their lines using motion capture technology, and in postproduction the actors were replaced with their CGI avatars, a literal stripping away of humanity. Cameron describes Avatar's manipulation with childlike glee: "If I want to fly through space, or change my perspective, I can. I can turn the whole scene into a living miniature…"[2] and explained the method of design as a "form of pure creation where if you want to move a tree or a mountain or the sky or change the time of day, you have complete control over the elements".[3] This godlike complex of digital creation is placing fictional creations before human emotion.

Star Wars director George Lucas is also guilty of dispensing with humanity in his films, the director's *Star Wars* prequel trilogy is awash with CGI worlds populated with CGI characters that interact with the human cast. Even in a situation where actors are in conversation with each other, Lucas employs digital tricks to cut and paste an actor's best take with the other actor's best take. Here Lucas strips away natural human interaction and replaces it with stiff and artificial interaction. Lucas has continually added digital layers to his original trilogy, inserting CGI characters, artificial action (Greddo shoots first!), and whole new backdrops to the original action. This has caused much uproar from fans of the original trilogy whose childhood imagination far outstripped the original films technological shortfall.

Not all have followed George Lucas and James Cameron's example. Christopher Nolan tried to fuse the scientific and humanistic with *Inception* (2010). *Inception* incorporated dazzling action set pieces and stunning visuals with a dream narrative that challenged the audience's perception of reality and dreams. However, Nolan's attempt to bring a more thoughtful approach to big budget filmmaking was for the most part unsuccessful. Despite its impressive ensemble cast and witty dialogue, *Inception* failed to garner a lasting emotional response from its audience. The mind-blowing effects and layered narrative stand like a fork in the road to an emotional response. Given that Nolan went out of his way to avoid using CGI, *Inception* adds digital layers, dressed up as human created dreamscapes, to compensate for the lack of human substance. This is no fault of Nolan's directorial skills; this is simply audience expectation of how they now wish to be engaged by film.

In his book *Everything Bad is Good for You* (2008), author Steven Johnson makes a case for how modern popular culture is apparently making us smarter and more engaged. When compared to television, film and literacy culture from twenty or thirty years ago Johnson's premise is strong. We have, in the last ten years or so, seen an increase in complex plot narratives, that once lounged comfortably in film, infiltrating mainstream television. Johnson takes his examples from a wider spectrum of media, but focus primarily on the popular television dramas *24, ER, Lost,* and *The Sopranos,* as well as looking at comedy programs like *Seinfeld.* Since Johnson's book was published an array of other television dramas have continued the trend of complex and multiple narratives that weave and thread from episode to season. *Game of Thrones, The Corner, Boardwalk Empire, Curb Your Enthusiasm,* and even video games such as *Grand Theft Auto,* all offer the audience an enormous amount of fat to chew on. Johnson points out that audience engagement with these programmes is paramount to giving the show mainstream appeal. Websites and blogs, magazines and television documentaries all vie to decipher the shows contents, narrative and dialogue, explain to casual viewers the heavy going dramas of *24's* Jack Bauer or the complex family politics of Tony Soprano. Television is beginning to engage audiences on a cognitive level that satisfies the human emotional range more than film can. Film is notable in its absence from Johnson's book as an example of how modern popular culture is engaging our brains.

For decades popular film has offered only visual thrills and in the last decade, as digital technology has become more efficient and widespread, the thrill has been replaced with a deafening roar of excessive and baffling visual effects. An example of this can be found in the Michael Bay directed *Transformers: Revenge of the Fallen* (2009), a film so riddled with visual CGI the plot of the movie is drowned under a barrage of twisting and scattering metal contraptions battling each other for screen space. The image has been described as "unrelenting. It's easy to walk away feeling like you've spent 2½ hours in the mad, wild hydraulic embrace of a car compactor".[4] It doesn't stop with *Transformers.* Films such as *Battle: LA* (2009) and *2012* (2010), have been criticized for the extensive use of digital effects over human narrative.

The difference between the Loudness War in music and film is that music listeners are revolting against the manipulation of the audio and demanding authenticity to their music. There are genuine campaigns battling the Loudness War in music, and demands are being made by the listener to bands and artists not to employ audio fakery to enhance the bombast of a song (turnmeup.org). The same cannot be said for the film audience. There are no active campaigns against the use of CGI, or visual manipulation in modern cinema; audiences are not demanding more engaging and complex narratives from major production studios. The only vocal concerns seem to stem from audiences of the original *Star Wars* trilogy who feel their childhood memories are being tampered with by the excessive use of digital re-mastering and CGI additions to the original films. This seems to be a solitary campaign that only extends to three films in particular; no demands are extended towards any other film. Modern blockbusters are lauded by critics and audiences for their use of digital layers, but this is strictly a visual compliment. The films fall short on an emotional level and offer only spectacle to compensate for the lack of humanity.

Published by *Gadfly*, April 2013

Postscript

Home Movies: A Critique of a Disappearing film and a Lingering Memory

In the summer of 2006 I made a feature length music documentary called *Home Movies*. The film profiled four bands from around the city of Leicester, UK. At the time I was working full-time in a bookstore, from which I made a living; and part-time as a filmmaker, from which I made no living whatsoever. I fancied myself something of an auteur, and tried to garner a fairly respectable reputation as a maverick of making films on the cheap. In retrospect, it was only when I began to try and make money from filmmaking that it started to fall apart. My "production company" at the time was called KillFilms, later morphing into the more professional and less nihilistic-sounding FrameDropFilms. After a while I started to get some serious offers: money exchanged hands, not big money, but some, and frankly, that's when the fun ended. The late nights, hanging in musty backrooms of venues and drinking the warm beer the venue manager had designated to the bands became less social and fun and more like work. With money involved, I felt I had to remain professional and coherent, whilst the bands and hangers-on lived it up in a less extravagant echo of rock 'n' roll debauchery. Thus, I'd leave a venue after midnight stone-cold sober and depressed, with tapes of uninspiring footage. I recoiled from the process, and admit that I found selling my so-called art a disheartening prospect. The films I made whilst being paid are not bad, but I'm happy to drop them from existence. I felt the lack of experimentation and daring I acquired whilst doing favours for bands and artists was lost in these more formal pieces. I still have many projects to be proud of from my excursion into filmmaking and one of those is *Home Movies*. The film achieved one film festival screening as a whole (of which I was a co-organizer anyway), and a short excerpt was screened at another arts festival. The sad thing is that *Home Movies* no longer exists in its original form. It is even dying on the one and only DVD on which I managed to burn it. I still own the individually edited band sections of the film as digital files, but the digital tapes the footage was recorded on have long vanished. In between each chapter was a minute or so montage of experimental image and sound, borrowed from numerous mediums, which has now been wiped from my memory and from my long defunct hard drive. Even the credit roll at the end of film is gone.

I was inspired to produce *Home Movies* after watching the documentary *Dig!* (2004), a film chronicling the rivalry between two bands: The Brian Jonestown Massacre and The Dandy Warhols. That film was intended by its filmmaker, Ondi Timoner, to profile a number of bands in the Portland, Oregon area. In the end *Dig!* sprawled into a seven year project and pulled focus on two of the most debauched, yet brilliant, bands in recent music history. I didn't see why Leicester was any different in musical potency to Portland, although we certainly lacked the drugs and booze-fuelled depravity, at least to my knowledge. The bands profiled in *Home Movies* had fifteen minutes of airtime; perhaps subconsciously I was thinking of Andy Warhol famous prediction of fifteen minutes of fame for everyone, or possibly, and more realistically, it was just convenient screen time. The bands included were Ambrose Tompkins, a three piece bunch of likely lads who wrote the most hummable lovely folk and vintage rock tunes (they still exist, but now as a one-man show with singer and guitarist Rob Waddington, whilst the other two members joined with the psychedelic pop band The Junipers). Tokyo Beatbox were a bunch of bright young things who wrote sharp and brash blasts of political and social punk pop, and whose live shows often climaxed with members of the audience dancing ring-a-ring-a-roses in front of the stage. Their sense of theatre was most profound. Tokyo Beatbox split and re-formed as Beat Fiction, only to sadly split once again after a few months. Canadian singer songwriter Dana Wylie and her band (the Dana Wylie Band) just happened to be living twenty miles away at the time of filming, and seemed like a natural choice to counter the male dominance of local music at the time. Her bluesy voice made it sound like she had come from the Deep South, not the cold north. She returned to Canada in 2008 where she is something of a star in the roots and blues underground. Finally there was the post-rock band, Her Name is Calla, whose sparse atmospherics would descend into bloody noise and a million screams. They gained moderate success in the UK and Europe, and are still going strong, although only one member remains from the line-up printed to screen in *Home Movies*. The bands were willing participants, at ease talking about their music and performing in front of my disintegrating digital cameras. They did not make any judgement calls on me regarding my rather amateurish approach to filmmaking.

After recently watching the only surviving and gradually decompiling DVD copy of *Home Movies,* I relived the excitement of filming and editing my own movie. The title sequence, though in retrospect, is mystifying. Crackling grain and the voice of CeeBee, played by Linda Manz from Dennis Hopper's 1980 film *Out of the Blue* proclaiming "Kill all hippies...Disco sucks". What was I trying to say? Was I trying to be sonically cool and obscure? I probably was. The film proper opens with Tokyo Beatbox launching into a live rendition of the joyous *For What it's Worth*, a song that in its recorded version still gives me an adrenaline rush and contains one of the truest lyrics ever written: "It was so much easier with a teenage chip on my shoulder", because let's be honest, weren't all things much easier that way? After the song finishes I start an interview with the four members that is cut short by a collapsing panel the band are seated on. This scene stays in the picture, because frankly, it's too funny to leave out.

Lyricist and Bass Player Gareth Watts talks about his influences and particularly bands whose sound develops over a period of three or four records; an opportunity that no band today is ever given.

After a montage of guitar and amplifier porn (a sequence that will return throughout the film, but with different guitars and amplifiers), lead guitarist Simon briskly walks the members through a new song *The Aftermath,* one that will turn up a year or so later when Tokyo Beatbox become Beat Fiction. The song is illustrated with footage of the band larking about and laughing. I wanted to give each band's chapter a piece of their recorded music (as opposed to my rickety camera's internal microphone recording live renditions). Luckily a month or two earlier, I had filmed Tokyo Beatbox at the legendary London venue The Bull and Gate and created a music video to their song *Maggie's Last Dance,* a song that glorified the demise of Margaret Thatcher (RIP). That video still shines with sheer pop gloss and fits in well with the rest of the documentary. Gareth has the last words of this segment: "There's no manifesto or agenda, if we fall into the same cliché, we want to do it gloriously… a glorious failure… which pretty much every minute feels like a glorious failure". (Aside: although they ultimately split as a band, Tokyo BeatBox did deserve fame and glory; their intelligence and energy punched through their music every time.) Then, a booming of a film reel running through a projector drowns him out and a wash of grainy, burning (fake) celluloid fills the screen, it continues until Dennis Hopper, of all people, shouts that he's an asshole, we are in *Out of the Blue* again with no reason why… but it's there.

Next, the film cuts out of the blue to footage of a lone black and white shot of a telegraph pole and a chorus of cartoon voices singing "you're the key to my heart" until a distorted crackle cuts them off and a breezy, summery tune jumps in. The Ambrose Tompkins segment is a blurry affair, literally in that the whole piece is so badly lit I had to up the contrast and colours of the footage in postproduction in order make any of it usable, hence the blur and extreme grain. Strangely the battered footage, recorded at Seamus Wong studios in Leicester, suits Ambrose Tompkins's rustic sound. I start the piece with an interview which like before is disrupted, but this time by drummer Ben Marshall dropping his roll up cigarette into his cup of tea. The snippets of music that we hear from Ambrose Tompkins in the first few moments offer promise of more to come, but for some strange reason I don't linger long enough for the viewer to appreciate the craft of the song. There is however enough of the bluesy gospel of *Running on Grass* to satisfy until it's cut abruptly to a vague interview question about the music scene around Leicester.

The first chance for Ambrose Tompkins to really shine is the recorded version of their song *This*, accompanied by footage of trees, overgrowth and rivers I shot, possibly a year earlier, whilst on a canal boat day trip with my parents. The footage has been treated in postproduction to a grain filter overhaul to make it look like it was filmed in some American backwater many decades ago. The footage from this quite lovely day trip with my parents has been long lost, so for me, this piece holds an additional few good memories of that day. We return to Ambrose Tompkins recorded live at a Leicester venue, The Musician. The footage is shaky from my nerves and the sound in the venue is hushed, thus the performance is muted. Perhaps trying to add a little drama, I end the piece just as Ambrose Tompkins is rollicking through a faster number with a freeze frame of each member and a barrage of gunshots. I deliberately stole this idea from the Rob Zombie horror film *The Devils Rejects* (2005), in which the bad guys are gunned down by police as Lynyrd Skynyrd's *Freebird* wails over the soundtrack, but the band didn't seem to mind their death scene. Not for the first time upon viewing, I am disappointed with this chapter. A year after the film was complete, this part was shown at a film and arts festival.

I remember it seeming longer than fifteen minutes and being slightly embarrassed about the unenthusiastic response. The blame for this chapter falls directly on me as director and not Ambrose Tompkins as the subjects. Although it appears as the second chapter, it was in fact the first footage I recorded for the film and so my nerves are easily on show.

The montage of footage and sound that separates Ambrose Tompkins and Dana Wylie Band is nothing but a flicker of clipped sounds. The DVD has been damaged and the source of the footage is now forgotten. I thought I heard a note from a song I once wrote myself, but I could be wrong. The Dana Wylie Band starts out strong with a song called *Hideout*, a real bluegrass ditty. I remember feeling nervous about travelling to Stamford (a small town about twenty five miles away from Leicester) where the band was living on a farm. Their recording space was, as I recall, a converted barn house and it was a bright and clear summer's day. This only served to add to the feeling I had left England and was now travelling in the American Deep South. By this point my camera is clearly breaking down, as the polarisation and blurring of the lens is not something I added in editing. *Hideout* ends with a distorted hiss and returns to band member Jez talking about a song they wrote for their album called *We Know the Secret*. The band performs this number a cappella: just handclaps and harmonies and it's glorious. I make the best decision of the entire film and do not cut to something else, but let the song play out in its entirety. My own 'whoop' of applause at the end of the song is genuine, and I remember clearly feeling at the time like I witnessed a truly special moment. I still think this now when re-watching the footage. The band is interesting and insightful in their interview pieces; Dana's Canadian twang adds a little dash of internationalism to proceedings. The recorded song *I Know You Know* is accompanied by footage I shot on the train on route to film the band, and shots of them walking around the farmyard. The Dana Wylie chapter of the film is the only one to not contain any footage that was shot elsewhere. At this point, the DVD is breaking apart as the Dana Wylie segment ends; lots of green dots and clipped sound violate the picture. The disk stops playing. I have to watch the next chapter on my computer. Much like the broken DVD the chapter ends with a broken camera. The lens bends and stretches the band across the screen and they vanish.

Her Name is Calla's section of the film is the artiest. The first shot is an empty picture frame on a beige wall where the band's name appears within. The creeping chords of *Hideous Box* fade in and footage of a sepia tinged Spanish mountain range flickers up intercut with black and white shots of the band playing the song live. Nostalgically, within this footage is a shot of band member Tom inhaling a cigarette and blowing smoke into the dark ether, of course smoking is the norm in most rock 'n' roll documentaries, but smoking inside bars was banned in the UK the following year and it's hard to remember a time when you could smoke indoors. The Spanish mountain footage was shot earlier the same year whilst on holiday in Malaga. If the audio of the steep gondola journey towards the mountain's peak had been retained, you would have heard my own fearful whimpers and proclamations of death as the little swinging gondola rattled along its ancient lines. Whatever mortal fear I suffered on the journey up the mountain, however, was worthwhile; not only was it breathtaking up there, but I secured footage that was just waiting for Her Name is Calla to soundtrack.

It was not entirely possible to get a coherent interview from Her Name is Calla, thus the interview segment is subtitled 'The Ramblings of Mad Men', but they offer clear insight into their future, and judging by the fair success they achieved in the UK and Europe, they were mostly right. Another special moment emerges within the film when Her Name is Calla perform *A Sleeper,* an alt-gospel song that made everyone at the gig sit down and clap along (a year or so later I would have the honour to 'sing' this song along with many others on a recorded version). The film ends with a bristling speaker-bursting live version of *Moment of Clarity*, the song's screamed refrain: "that sound is the crunch of the human spirit breaking" is accompanied by a re-digitized copy of an experimental film I made years earlier, pretentiously titled *Subconscious Abstraction* (itself lifted from a lyric by British band Manic Street Preachers). The section ends with a volley of shouts and claps from the audience as the band lay down their instruments and walk off the stage, a move I asked them to do for finality's sake, possibly the only bit of direction I gave in the entire film.

As mentioned previously, *Home Movies* no longer exists. As I wrote this piece the last DVD copy I had of the movie decompiled, and will, therefore, never be playable again. I could remake it using the band documentaries and stitch them together using sound bites from *Out of the Blue*, but parts of that film are unrecoverable, so it will never be the same film again, and what would be the point anyway? Nostalgia for a time when both I and the bands included were younger, possibly dumber and more care free then we are today is not a good enough reason to try and put the pieces back in the puzzle. We have all moved on. *Home Movies* is over and my filmmaking days are also over. Like real home movies, the memory of those times is always better than reliving it on screen.

On reflection, *Home Movies* is something of an aesthetic failure. The use of postproduction film grain drapes the film in a false nostalgia, and whilst the experimental elements might appear arty and obscure, they in fact add nothing to the overall narrative of the film. However, with regard to some of the themes discussed in this book, *Home Movies* was a triumph, an example of artistic individuality and vision. The fact that the film was made on a zero budget, with a decrepit digital camera and edited on cheap editing software, yet still was coherent and absorbing, slaps capitalism in the face and makes for a rewarding human endeavor. As bewildering as the film might be to me personally six years after, it was a satisfying experience to watch and know that I was solely responsible for its occasional victories, as well as the majority of its flaws. *Home Movies* is not perfect, but my argument is that film shouldn't be perfect. As an audience we should accept and even demand that films have faults, because that is the truism of our everyday lives. We should be compelled to turn our backs on cold digitally created worlds, that can be tampered and adjusted on a whim (yes, that does mean you George Lucas) and instead delve into worlds that are a reflection of us: imperfect, yet striving; at fault, but aware; living within the moment, yet constantly seeking change. Contemporary American cinema has glossed over our existence with sleek unreality, which, ultimately, will lead us nowhere.

Individual documentaries from *Home Movies* can be found here:
    http://www.youtube.com/watch?v=BW6dkumuZIk&list=PLm AmIZNxgyDG-6ayL7BcI-8UcwOAnsKuY

Notes

Commando, Arnold Schwarzenegger and U.S Foreign Policy

1 Kornbluh, Peter. "Still Hidden: A Full Record Of What the U.S. Did in Chile." *www.hartford-hwp.com*. N.p., 24 Oct. 1999. Web. 4 Oct. 2012.

2 Arnold Schwarzenegger 2004 Republican National Convention Address." *www.americanrhetoric.com*. N.p., 31 Aug. 2004. Web. 09 June 2013.

The Easy Rider Paradox

1 Hunter, Jack. "Out of the Blue." *Dennis Hopper: Movie Top Ten*. London: Creation, 1999. p.87. Print.

2 All Sources: *Internet Movie Data Base*. IMDb.com, n.d. Web. 18 Dec. 2012.

3 Orlean, Matthieu. "Photoghaphy, Writing, Acting ... Movie-making had Everything in One Package." In *Dennis Hopper and the New Hollywood*. Flammarion, 2009. p.126. Print.

Nobody Puts America in the Corner: Dirty Dancing and the End of Innocence

1 Leary, Timothy. *Flashbacks: A Personal and Cultural History of an Era : An Autobiography*. Los Angeles: J.P. Tarcher, 1990. p.253. Print.

Digital Socialism: How Mumblecore Filmmaking is Defying Capitalism

1 All Sources. *Internet Movie Data base*. IMDb.com, n.d. Web. 26 Jan. 2012.

2 Marx, Karl and Friedrich Engels. "Manifesto of the

Communist Party." *Http://www.marxists.org/*. n.d. Web. 16 Mar. 2013.

North Korea in Fiction and as Fiction

1   Totilo, Stephen. "China Is Both Too Scary and Not Scary Enough To Be Video Game Villains." *Kotaku.com*. N.p., 13 Jan. 2011. Web. 5 Jan. 2013.
2   Kim, Jong-Il,. *The Cinema and Directing*. Pyongyang, Korea: Foreign Languages Pub. House, 1987. p.5. Print.

How to Make a Film in North Korea...If you had to

1   Pulver, Andrew. "UK Film-makers Divided on David Cameron's Support for Box-office Hits." *The Guardian*. Guardian News and Media, 01 Dec. 2012. Web. 17 Feb. 2013.
2   Juche Ideology." *Http://www.korea-dpr.com*. N.p., 2011. Web. Jan.-Feb. 2013.
3   Kim Jong-Il. *The Cinema and Directing*. Pyongyang, Korea: Foreign Languages Pub. House, 1987. p.7. Print.
4   *ibid*, p.10. Print.
5   *ibid*, p.9. Print.
6   *ibid*, p.12. Print.

Louder than War: Have Movies Fallen into the same Loudness Trap as Music?

1   Michaels, Sean. "Death Magnetic 'loudness war' rages on." *The Guardian*. Guardian News and Media, 01 Oct. 2008. Web. 17 Mar. 2013.
2   Waxman, Sharon. "Computers Join Actors In Hybrids On Screen." *The New York Times*. N.p., 09 Jan. 2007. Web. 17 Mar. 2013.
3   Warren, Jane. "Avatar: Director James Cameron's Crowning

Glory." *Daily Express Films RSS*. N.p., 11 Dec. 2009. Web. 15 June 2013.

4 Sharkey, Betsy. "Transformers: Revenge of the Fallen" *Los Angeles Times*. Los Angeles Times, 24 June 2009. Web. 15 Apr. 2013.

Contemporary culture has eliminated both the concept of the public and the figure of the intellectual. Former public spaces – both physical and cultural – are now either derelict or colonized by advertising. A cretinous anti-intellectualism presides, cheerled by expensively educated hacks in the pay of multinational corporations who reassure their bored readers that there is no need to rouse themselves from their interpassive stupor. The informal censorship internalized and propagated by the cultural workers of late capitalism generates a banal conformity that the propaganda chiefs of Stalinism could only ever have dreamt of imposing. Zer0 Books knows that another kind of discourse – intellectual without being academic, popular without being populist – is not only possible: it is already flourishing, in the regions beyond the striplit malls of so-called mass media and the neurotically bureaucratic halls of the academy. Zer0 is committed to the idea of publishing as a making public of the intellectual. It is convinced that in the unthinking, blandly consensual culture in which we live, critical and engaged theoretical reflection is more important than ever before.